DESIGN TO
GROW

How Coca-Cola Learned
to Combine
Scale and Agility
(and How You Can Too)

DAVID BUTLER
AND
LINDA TISCHLER

SIMON & SCHUSTER

New York London Toronto Sydney New Delhi

Simon & Schuster
1230 Avenue of the Americas
New York, NY 10020

First Simon & Schuster hardcover edition February 2015

SIMON & SCHUSTER and colophon are registered trademarks of
Simon & Schuster, Inc.

For information about special discounts for bulk purchases, please
contact Simon & Schuster Special Sales at 1-866-506-1949 or
business@simonandschuster.com.

The Simon & Schuster Speakers Bureau can bring authors to your live
event. For more information or to book an event, contact the Simon
& Schuster Speakers Bureau at 1-866-248-3049 or visit our website at
www.simonspeakers.com.

Illustrations on pages 142 and 143 by Rory Panagotopulos
Interior design by Ellen R. Sasahara

Manufactured in the United States of America

1   3   5   7   9   10   8   6   4   2

Library of Congress Cataloging-in-Publication Data

Butler, David (Designer)
Design to grow : how Coca-Cola learned to combine scale and agility
(and how you can too) / David Butler, Linda Tischler.
pages cm
1. Technological innovations—Management. 2. Organizational
effectiveness. 3. Strategic planning. 4. Entrepreneurship. 5. Coca-Cola
Company. I. Tischler, Linda. II. Title.
HD45.B88 2015
658.4'063—dc23
2014029755

ISBN 978-1-4516-7182-7
ISBN 978-1-4516-7627-3 (ebook)

For Allen, Claudia, Stelle, and Ruby—I'm a lucky man. David

For Hank, Melissa, and Ben—I'm thrice blessed. Linda

"If you want to build a ship, don't drum up the men to gather wood, divide the work, and give orders. Instead, teach them to yearn for the vast and endless sea."

—Antoine de Saint-Exupéry

Contents

Preface

S CALE AND AGILITY. In today's volatile and rapidly changing world, these are the two essentials that every company needs to grow and remain relevant.

If you're a big, established company, you've got scale, which enables you to expand almost effortlessly from Boston to Bangalore. Over time, you've built up powerful assets—expertise, brands, customers, distribution channels, relationships—that most startups could only dream about. Scale is not your problem. Your problem is agility—you must be smarter, faster, leaner than the startup that's got your industry in its crosshairs—targeted for disruption.

How can you grow (gain market share, increase your brand's relevance, and generate revenue growth) with the speed and flexibility of a startup? Every big, established company, organization, and even government is at risk of being disrupted, having a so-called Kodak Moment, watching its industry upended and its competitive advantages—the moats that have protected it for decades—disappear overnight.

If you're in a startup, you've got a different problem. You've got agility, actually, nothing but agility. Trying new business models, repositioning your company, developing new features, or even whole new products, within days—things big companies can only dream about—are not your problem. For you, building the right team, deciding which metrics matter, acquiring customers, and securing funding are what keep you up at night. Scale is your problem—doing what it takes to expand your startup into new geographies, including the land of profitability, is your challenge. That's why most startups fail—only a dispiriting one out of ten succeeds.

What if there were something that could help you grow, avoid disruption, and even take giant steps forward? What if there were something that could help you create both scale and/or agility?

There is—it's called *design*.

And that's what this book is about—how The Coca-Cola Company uses design to grow, and how the lessons it learned can help other companies, regardless of size, industry, or geography, do the same.

For over a century, Coca-Cola has used design to scale to over two hundred countries, build seventeen billion-dollar brands, partner with more than twenty million retail customers, and sell close to two billion products a day. But the company is still learning. Over the last decade, it has focused on mastering how also to use design to create agility—something most established companies, including Coca-Cola, struggle with.

We'll deconstruct this journey by demystifying the often confusing language of design into a set of plain-spoken, easy-to-understand principles. Along the way, we'll explore examples from around the world and across different parts of the company—mango growing in Kenya, packaging in Tokyo, retail shops in Bogotá, advertising in Cape Town, and social fountain machines in the United States—to make it easier to understand the role design can play in helping one of the largest companies on the planet become nimbler and more adaptable to a complex and changing world. The stories themselves may be unique to Coca-Cola, but the challenges they describe are universal.

How to use this book

A few words about how this book is organized. Part 1 explains how to design for scale, and shows how The Coca-Cola Company used design across its business to create a $170 billion, global brand.

In chapter 1 we grapple with the question, *What is design?* then show how design creates value and what it looks like to design on purpose.

In chapter 2, we investigate how The Coca-Cola Company used design strategically to scale Coca-Cola into one of the most, if not *the* most, ubiquitous brands on the planet.

In chapter 3, we look at three realities that create the new normal of today's marketplace: wicked problems, the changes unleashed by the after-Internet world, and the need to create shared value. There are, of course, other factors, but these three have created a new level of external complexity, challenging every company's ability to grow.

In part 2, we discuss what it takes to join the Billion-Dollar Brand Club, and explore why it's getting harder than ever for established companies to maintain their status as part of this elite group. We'll examine how startups design for agility and how big, established companies can too.

In chapter 4, we'll explain how design can actually help any company learn to fail fast, and adapt to stay ahead of the competition. We'll show how The Coca-Cola Company uses design to create adaptability from its 5-Note Melody to its manual distribution systems in Africa to the redesign of hundreds of bodegas in Latin America.

In chapter 5, we'll see how designing modular systems is one way for a company to stay agile enough to survive and thrive. We'll look at three examples from Coca-Cola: its global juice visual identity system, a high-density mango growing initiative, and the development of the Freestyle drink machine, to see how designing modular systems really works.

In chapter 6, we see why designing open systems, such as Wikipedia, allows for greater collaboration, both within a company and with a company's stakeholders. That process, it turns out, can not only help in uncovering the best talent and ideas, but can result in cost savings along the way. We look at the development of the Coca-Cola Design Machine, its 5by20 global commitment to empower women entrepreneurs, and its initiatives around global water use as examples of open systems in action.

Finally, in the epilogue, we consider what the future will look like in a world where design is democratized. We'll also explore what big companies can learn from startups to help them avoid significant disruption, and what startups can learn from big companies that would let them beat that dismal startup failure rate. Will the next wave of innovation—building scale-ups—be the answer for both ends of the business spectrum?

Throughout the book, we offer lessons that any company can use to grow and thrive, along with suggestions as to how you can use our road-tested ideas for getting everybody in your company on board.

In The Deep End, we provide references for anyone who wants to delve further into the ideas presented here, as well as the never-before-published "Designing on Purpose" manifesto that was my Jerry Maguire moment at the company, and the seed for this book.

In the course of this book, we'll go behind the scenes of The Coca-Cola Company's operations, ranging from how the carpet industry helped it make the decision on what shade of blue to use for the Dasani bottle to how it's turning local biowaste—from sugar cane stalks in Brazil to tree bark in Russia—into PlantBottle Packaging.

Most of these problems are, of course, specific to Coca-Cola, but every business can learn from the way the company used design to solve them.

PART 1

Designing for Scale

T he first week of November 2013 saw a flurry of unusually compelling stories in the business news. Tesla suffered another battery fire, prompting fears of a recall. The Feds nailed a hedge-fund titan with a fondness for insider trading. The stock market hit a new high. However, even amid such provocative headlines, two events stood out: the shuttering of a once-mighty retail empire, and the stratospheric stock market debut of a seven-year-old Internet darling.

Blockbuster, which made standing in line to rent a video the first stop in millions of movie lovers' weekend plans, finally called it quits. A day later, Twitter, a favorite with celebrities, revolutionaries, and the occasional misguided politician, ended its first day with a market cap of $30B: more than Kellogg's, Whole Foods, and half the firms in the S&P 500.

That was a rather extraordinary week, but it was also a great snapshot of today's marketplace—both the risk and the opportunity that come with industry disruption. In today's world of hyperconnectivity and exponential growth, every company is stepping back to evaluate where it's vulnerable or how it can find an edge and revolutionize an industry.

It's not enough to be big: At its peak, Blockbuster had about 9,000 retail stores across the United States. It had the scale but not the agility to remain relevant. And, while every founder dreams of creating the next Twitter or Instagram, 90 percent of companies won't live to see year two. While they're all designed to be agile, most of them struggle with scale.

Every company needs both scale and agility to win.

From a fledgling startup in Nepal to a century-old multinational in New York, scale and agility are two things that are essential to every company's success.

Scale and Agility

If you're working for a startup, you *get* agility. Chances are, you're iterating your product/market fit daily, and pivoting when necessary, just to stay alive. But the thing that keeps you up at night is *scale*— stabilizing your business model, so that you can move to the next stage and become a company. This requires more funding, more staff, more customers, more of everything.

If you're working for an established company, you *get* scale: In fact, the reason you're in the position you're in is because you know how a company at scale operates. You're successful because you know how to leverage scale with a high degree of effectiveness and efficiency. Perhaps you'd like to grow revenue or expand operations, but what you worry about is keeping up and staying competitive in a world of increasing uncertainty and change, complicated by the upstarts searching for ways to disrupt your industry.

If your company is public, you understand all of this in a different dimension. You live under the pressure of managing a global business every day, knowing that at the end of the quarter you and your peers will be ruthlessly judged by thousands of stakeholders. There are millions—and sometimes billions—of dollars at risk every quarter. Managing your scale is always a concern but what keeps you up at night is mainly *agility*—how to meet expectations this quarter but also create the speed and flexibility your company needs to drive innovation and create the culture you need to remain relevant to the next generation.

As vice president of Innovation and Entrepreneurship at The Coca-Cola Company, and former head of design, I'm often asked questions like, "How does Coca-Cola, a hundred-year-old brand, stay relevant?" And, "How does a giant company like Coca-Cola innovate? What's your strategy?"

What if there were something that you—your startup, your team, your function, your division—could use to create the kind of scale and agility you need to win?

Design can create both scale and agility.

When it comes to design, most people want to know the basics: "How does Coca-Cola use design to stay competitive?" "How do you create the most value from design?" "How do you use design to innovate?" These are all good questions, since even the most analytical and execution-oriented business managers know that design can create value far beyond just making products look and feel better. For some companies, design can actually help them grow. But how?

Coca-Cola and Design

When you think of Coca-Cola and design, your mind probably goes immediately to the company's most iconic brand—Coca-Cola—with its familiar color, distinctive logo, and iconic packaging. The combination of those elements, designed over a century ago, helped create one of the world's most valuable brands, worth over $170 billion.

However, at Coca-Cola, design is about more than the traditional, and visible, elements. While logos and colors are important, it's the stuff you can't see, the stuff that's invisible, that's often doing the heavy lifting.

Coca-Cola designs things like products, advertising, packaging, and coolers, as well as the way those things connect to each other to drive growth. And that's what makes the way Coca-Cola designs *strategic*.

When used strategically, design can help companies grow.

Most people don't think about design this way, but things that are well designed are actually well *connected* and part of a system. For example, when Coca-Cola designs a new package, its goal is to actually solve business problems, not simply to pick colors, specify materials, or determine its shape and size.

All those things are important, but the new package must also connect to its supply-chain strategy, help the company meet its sustainability goals, work within the constraints of its bottling and distribution system, fit well with its retail customers' business plans, and, of course, meet the needs of its consumers. When all these things connect, we'd say that the company is using design strategically to help it grow.

The Invisible Drives the Visible

I love systems and exploring the ways in which systems work. Most systems aren't readily apparent: For example, you don't think of your kid's school bus, your local grocery store, or an app on your smart phone, as parts of big systems, but they are. Understanding how systems work can really change the way you see the world.

In 1995, my wife turned me on to a book by systems guru Peter Senge, *The Fifth Discipline*. I remember reading, "Systems thinking is a discipline for seeing wholes. It is a framework for seeing interrelationships rather than things, for seeing patterns of change rather than static snapshots."

That book started me on a journey of learning everything I could about systems and their relationship to design. I became consumed with the interrelationship of things more than the design of individual pieces of the whole, as Senge would put it. I became fascinated with many different types of systems and their effects on the world—from systemic risk (economics) to chaos theory (science). I wanted to know everything about how systems work—especially big, complex systems.

In 2004, I joined The Coca-Cola Company. My mandate was to help the company focus on design: to develop a vision, strategy, and approach to ensure it was getting the most value out of design.

I was stoked; I saw the company itself as a giant system made up of hundreds of subsystems. I couldn't wait to dig in.

It didn't take long to see why the company wanted to concentrate on this area. The Coca-Cola Company owns some of the most valuable and well-known brands in the world, including Coca-Cola, Diet Coke, Sprite, and Fanta. However, at that time it didn't have a consistent approach to the way it designed. This created many little disconnects across the way in which people experienced its brands, from packaging to communications to retail. It needed to get back to the level of quality, consistency, and leadership that the company's brands were known for.

It also needed a way to adapt more quickly to a rapidly changing market. The nonalcoholic, ready-to-drink industry has consistently been one of the fastest growing consumer industries in the world. In order to keep pace with the market, Coca-Cola needed a way to use design to remain relevant, nimble, and adaptable to change. But it was clear that it didn't yet have it.

All these little disconnects were starting to make the company's brands feel old and outdated when compared with other fast-moving consumer brands like Apple and Nike. As a company, Coca-Cola was designing at massive scale, but a lot of the things weren't connected to each other. That made it very difficult to drive the company's growth strategy. The way Coca-Cola was designing was actually working *against* its own interests.

Sure, it needed to work on the things that were very visible—packaging, advertising, websites, trucks, and coolers. But it needed to focus on its approach—the way it designed as a company—first.

The way Coca-Cola had used design in the past wasn't giving it the agility it needed to grow in a rapidly changing and connected world.

The company's business had become very complex, yet its approach to design had been conceived for a much simpler organization. There's nothing simple about a company with a network of more than 250 bottling companies, 80,000 suppliers, and 20 million retail customers. However, when you look at how the company evolved, it's easy to see why it was hard to let go of an approach that had worked so well for so long.

For its first seventy years, The Coca-Cola Company had had one brand, one product, one package size, and, for the most part, one price. For more than seven decades, Coca-Cola sold for just five cents. The company's growth strategy was to scale Coca-Cola to every country, city, town, and village—to put Coca-Cola "within arm's reach of desire" of every person on the planet. Amazingly, that's pretty much what happened.

Then, in 1982, the company took a risk and launched Diet Coke. That made its business more complicated. For the first time, there were two Cokes in its portfolio. Diet Coke quickly became a huge success, so any difficulties were more than made up for in sales.

In 2001, Coca-Cola upped the ante by making a big strategic decision, to become a *total beverage company*, meaning that it wanted to provide a much wider variety of options in line with changing attitudes and tastes. This changed everything, from its product portfolio to how the system (the term Coca-Cola uses to represent the company and its network of over 250 independent bottling companies) operates.

Coca-Cola's CEO at the time told a British newspaper that the company's goal was not only to develop the systems needed for success in a globalized economy, but to be equally sensitive as to how it operates locally. Internally, that strategy was distilled down to a pithy shorthand: "Think globally and act locally." Each business unit ran its business independently, keeping the pedal to the metal on its global brands, but also leveraging the company's international scale to create or acquire regional and local brands as well.

However, this shift in strategy begat something Coca-Cola hadn't anticipated—enormous complexity.

The decision to go from being a one-brand company to a total-beverage company in a world of dramatic technological, social, and political change created a level of complexity that was unprecedented. This kind of monumental shift in business strategy also required a shift in the company's approach to design.

Originally, its approach was to make everything as easy as possible to scale; Coca-Cola used design to simplify, standardize, and integrate its business, which made it much easier to drive its growth strategy. That's essentially how The Coca-Cola Company grew from a little startup in 1886 to a company valued at over $120 billion in 2001.

However, it couldn't use this same approach to design for a company that now had hundreds of brands, products, and packages; thousands of suppliers; and millions of distribution channels, ranging from big box superstores to guys with coolers standing underneath umbrellas in the street. The same design strategy would no longer work for a product portfolio that ranged from sparkling beverages to coffee drinks to dozens of juices.

Coca-Cola needed an approach that would help it to leverage its scale but *also* help create more flexibility and adaptability across its business.

By 2002, its business was really complicated. It was clear that there was a problem. In April of that same year, *Time* magazine released an article with a headline that summed up what most people were thinking: "Has Coke Lost Its Fizz?"

Coca-Cola had a business problem, but what most people couldn't see was how it was related to design. The realization that the two were inextricably connected wasn't some kind of grand epiphany or big *aha* in the boardroom. For decades, the company had used design to build a multinational, multibillion dollar business almost intuitively. However, at that moment, Coca-Cola hadn't been able to harness that capability as effectively as it had in the past.

Jerry Maguire and Me

This is where things stood when I joined the company. Soon after I arrived, I knew that we needed a much bigger change than I had imagined—the company needed to *redesign* the way it designed. And I also knew that to do this—to shift the whole company's approach to design—everyone would have to *become designers*. They would have to see themselves as designers and learn how the decisions they made every day were related and could actually help us use design to win— to help the company grow. To be honest, I knew what we had to do; I just didn't know how to do it.

One day, as I was reading Rick Warren's book, *The Purpose-Driven Life*, I began connecting a few dots in his philosophy to the transformation I could imagine for design at The Coca-Cola Company. The basic question Warren's book asks is this: If, when you look at your life in full, from beginning to end, are you using your time on earth to *live on purpose*? Are you using your time to do something meaningful?

Before I read that book, I hadn't really thought about the idea of linking *purpose* (the real meaning behind what we were doing) with design, but then it all fell into place. Suddenly, I felt like I needed to write something—a story, a white paper, a manifesto, to connect the dots. I was having a "Jerry Maguire" moment.

If you've seen the movie, you remember Maguire's epiphany. I didn't stay up all night or run to Kinko's in the morning like Jerry, but my intensity could have come out of Maguire's playbook. I sat at my desk and began to write. By the end of the day, I had written a three-page paper called "Building Brands, by Design." It attempted to make the connection between what we were doing around the world— designing literally billions of things—from packaging to coolers to different kinds of marketing communications to websites to retail environments to licensed merchandise to trucks—with our business challenges and how we could use design as a powerful enabler of growth.

At the time, Coca-Cola, our flagship brand, which represents over 50 percent of the company's revenue, was languishing. Internally, it's often said that Coca-Cola is the oxygen of the company; it creates a halo effect on our whole portfolio of brands. When it's not doing well, everything else suffers. When it's growing, there's a trickle-down effect to other brands.

The company's design revolution had to start with Coca-Cola.

I knew that to demonstrate a new way of thinking about design we couldn't start with a smaller brand in our portfolio. We had to start with Coca-Cola. If we could make the link between growing Coca-Cola and design, we could do anything we wanted to after that; we'd have the confidence and proven results that we needed to create systemic change.

From the first page of the manifesto, I tried to help everyone understand how design could play a more significant role.

I mapped out my big idea and called it "designing on purpose."

Designing on purpose refers to design that is strategic, with a clear connection to our growth strategy; design that creates scale and agility—across markets and media; and design that inspires people. Designing on purpose should ultimately be design that leads culture.

I went on to recognize other companies that used design strategically: McDonald's, for the way it used its visual identity system to help integrate the organization; Apple, which used design as its competitive differentiator; Nike, which used design to build its reputation; and Volkwagen, which used design to create a cultlike corporate culture.

The third page focused on five strategies we could use to start designing on purpose. It went on to describe how different functions inside the organization could implement these strategies to begin to create a common approach to design across the company.

The point was clear: Design was not an esoteric discipline owned by an elite team at corporate headquarters, but an everyday responsibility that extended to every functional area of the company, in every region, on every brand. In order to get the maximum value from design, we each had a role to play.

I ended the manifesto with: "The opportunity is huge. The opportunity is now. Is using design as a strategic advantage an opportunity or our responsibility? We could and should be the company that other companies use as their standard for great design. We need to design on purpose."

The passion in that document would have brought tears to Renée Zellweger's eyes. I could envision her whispering: "You had me at 'strategic.'"

I remember finishing the paper, and sending it in an email to basically everyone I had met at the company (and many more that I hadn't) in the highest levels of management.

In retrospect, I'm still shocked at my own audacity. In a less tolerant organization, I could have been sacked like Jerry for sheer brass coupled with hopeless naïveté.

Fortunately, instead of being summoned to Human Resources to hand in my badge, something remarkable happened. The idea caught on. Before long, people began using that phrase—designing on purpose—for what we were doing. There wasn't any magic in those particular words or that particular document but, somehow, it was the right thing at the right time to get things started.

Redesigning Design

That simple three-page document kick-started almost a decade of designing on purpose at The Coca-Cola Company. Over time, we introduced a systems-based approach to design. This would give us both the consistency we needed to design at scale and the agility we were lacking to quickly adapt to a rapidly changing world. Now, we didn't do all of this overnight; it was a journey based on learning by doing.

We began with an area that most people could easily understand—branding and communications. We then moved to packaging and equipment. Then, we tackled retail experiences. Finally, we expanded the approach deeper into the operations of the business, into our distribution system and supply chain.

However, what really made the difference was opening up design to everyone, every function, and every geography. Our goal was to change how everyone designed—to make everyone a *designer* using a common approach—no matter what his or her title was.

During that period, the world also changed, with challenges we could have never envisioned a decade earlier, from the rise of social media, to ingredient scarcity, global economic chaos, geo-political instability, environmental sustainability issues, and the rise of China and the rest of the BRICs (Brazil, Russia, and India) into a new global middle class.

Still, the past decade has, by and large, been a good one for the company. It's added ten billion-dollar brands to its portfolio and doubled its stock price. Coca-Cola is on a trajectory to double the size of its business by 2020, essentially replicating in the space of a decade what took the company one hundred years to build.

Of course, design isn't the only factor that's created this kind of growth, but it is an important one. What most people don't realize is how Coca-Cola's approach to design has evolved over the past century, and particularly over the past decade, to make this happen.

Design is powerful. Once you understand how design creates value, and decide to design on purpose, you can unlock the power of design to drive both scale and agility. It's worked for Coca-Cola; it can for you, too.

CHAPTER 1

Design

The dumbest mistake is viewing design as something you do at the end of the process to "tidy up" the mess, as opposed to understanding it's a "day one" issue and part of everything.

Tom Peters

I f you ever thought growing *your* business was tough, try selling water.

In first-world countries, clean, drinkable water is ubiquitous and, for the most part, feels free. Turn on the tap, and you're good to go.

What's more, most people think water basically tastes the same no matter where you live. *Eau de Grand Rapids,* in their minds, is not that much different from *Stuttgart H2O.* Hardly a potential business model there.

Put it in a bottle, however, and suddenly you've got something: It's convenient. In developed countries, when people are on the go, many like to take their water with them: phone, keys, water, check. In developing countries, where most tap water is not safe to drink, bottled water is critical. It's essential for everything from cooking to brushing teeth. Bottles give water economic potential.

In the past decade, bottled water has become big business all around the world.

For a beverage company, that makes it an attractive addition to a portfolio. Compared to, say, juice, being in the bottled water business seems simple. No weather catastrophes, no crop diseases, no worries about bee colony collapse. But it's not. The margins are razor thin, and differentiating your brand is extremely difficult.

So, if you're in the bottled water business, the way you design everything from your supply chain to your packaging is critical. Design can create a *powerful* competitive advantage.

You may be surprised that a company best known for billion-dollar sparkling brands like Coca-Cola, Sprite, and Fanta also has two billion-dollar *water* brands. But, then, few people know that Coca-Cola's portfolio includes over 3,500 products, ranging from milk to juice to coffee, with over five hundred brands, such as Core Power, Qoo, and Love Body.

Around the globe, the company owns about one hundred water brands, including Dasani in the United States, Bonaqua in Hong Kong, Ciel in Mexico, and Kropla Beskido in Poland. Even though the main ingredient in all of Coca-Cola's products is water, it was a relative late-comer to the bottled water business. However, with its bottling capacity and distribution network, it was a logical category for the company to move into.

Bottled water subsequently has become one of the company's most significant businesses. Coca-Cola sold 5.8 billion liters of bottled water abroad and 253 million liters in the United States and Canada from 2007 to 2012.

Even for a company as big as Coca-Cola, creating competitive advantage for its water brands is an ongoing challenge.

Several years ago, in Japan, for example, its biggest brand of water, Minaqua, began showing signs of fatigue. It had never been a rock star in the company's portfolio but had chugged along delivering reliable results for a long time. Yet, over the years, Minaqua's market share had gradually dropped to the lowest in the category. In 2010, the company decided to do something about it. It wasn't clear what was to blame: Price? Availability? Packaging? Advertising? Customer relationships? A survey of the business yielded the most dispiriting of answers: "Likely, all of the above."

It's at this point—when different elements of your business don't connect to drive your growth strategy— that a business problem turns into a design problem.

That may be a surprising assertion, if you think of design only in terms of the color of the label or shape of the package. Those are all important, but design also has a much greater capacity to help your business if you think of it as the thread that connects all the dots. Once you get beneath the surface, and understand how design can help make all of the aspects of your business relate to each other, you can begin to really understand its power.

Before we talk about how Coca-Cola tackled the myriad, interconnected problems plaguing Minaqua, let's drop back for a moment and get clear on one of the most frustrating issues bedeviling any discussion of design. Namely, what, exactly, *is* it?

What Is Design?

Put this book down for a minute and look around you. Maybe you're reading this in a cozy armchair in your living room, or in the scrunched middle seat of an airplane. No matter. Survey your surroundings as if you were an archeologist who just unearthed all the things in your environment from the bottom of a pit.

Everything you see is designed by somebody.

That coffee mug you're holding, or the plastic cup holding your airline O.J., the lamp beside the chair or the one above your seat, the chair itself, the tray table, the ottoman, the carton the orange juice came from, the pattern of the fabric on the seat, the uniforms of the flight crew, the plane's engines, the gizmo that controls the entertainment center—all have been designed by somebody.

Most of us don't design smart phones, electric cars, or skyscrapers, but each of us designs stuff every day. We design meetings, presentations, deals, our plans for the weekend, the configuration of stuff on our (literal and virtual) desktops, children's birthday parties, the menu for dinner, and so on. In fact, we're all *designers*—we all design, all the time. It's just that each of us is better at designing some things than others.

Most people understand that there's a difference between good and bad design. And the same goes for companies—most people understand that companies are also better at designing some things better than others. So the challenge is not whether or not we *should* design.

The challenge, for all of us, is to design better—to get the most value out of the way we design.

However, is that possible? Can regular people—people without the word *design* in their title—really understand the difference between good and bad design so they, or their team or company, can actually be better designers? The answer is an unqualified *Yes!*

LESSON LEARNED #1

Start by Losing the D word

The word *design* can mean a lot of things to a lot of people. But design is just a means to an end, not the end.

After my first few months at the company, I tried to stop using the word *design* as much as possible. It just got in the way of the conversation.

Instead, I tried engaging people on things that drive our business and talked about the impact that design could make, stuff that everybody was interested in and could understand. We found we had lots to discuss.

Here's the point: The precise language you use to talk about design is not important. The critical thing is to communicate the value that design can create by connecting things to solve a problem. If using more familiar language is part of that, don't sweat it. There's nothing magical about words like *user-centered*, *hierarchy*, or *interaction*. (If you don't have *design* in your title, chances are these words don't mean anything to you anyway. Don't worry about it.)

When I'm talking to a group of people internally—marketers, finance people, sales guys, accountants, or even some of our scientists, I focus on how design creates value. I try to stay focused on how things connect, in *their* world, to better understand design.

I often ask people to think about their favorite restaurant. Sure, the food is probably good. But is that enough to make you keep going back? What about the look and feel of the place? What's the atmosphere like? The comfort of the seats? How about the view? The friendliness of the staff? Do they remember your name? Is the menu easy to read, even by candlelight? How about the plates, or the utensils, or the tables? Can you easily book online, or find the latest specials on the Web site? Is it easy to park? Are the acoustics such that you can actually hold a conversation without shouting? Any one of these things is necessary, but not sufficient. Connect them all and you likely have a very successful restaurant.

You can use your own examples from your favorite vacation, your favorite car, or the house you most enjoyed living in. Design played an important role because lots of things seemed to fit together seamlessly—maybe even intuitively—to the point at which you didn't even really have to think about it. And that's how design creates value.

By losing so-called designy language, you are forced to come up with other metaphors for what you're describing, tailored to the audience you're addressing. And that, in and of itself, is by design.

Key Takeaway: The language of design can be confusing and alienating to a lot of people. There's no magic in design lingo and no reason to be wedded to it. Substitute language that works for the group you're addressing if it helps everybody understand.

It's easy to know the difference between good and bad design.

Let's go back to our discussion of the designed elements you see every time you get on an airplane. If airline travel is part of your job, you likely know which airlines have better seats than others. If you're like me, you've thought about the way your seat was designed. I often ask myself questions like, "Why did they put the button here?" "Do I really have to go through all these steps just to be able to turn on the light?" Or, "Doesn't anybody ever try *sitting* in these before they install them?" (Okay, if I'm honest, I've used stronger language—especially when it took me more than five minutes to find the electrical outlet.)

If you've ever done this, you've evaluated the design of the seat without even thinking about it—you've determined if the seat was *good* or *bad* design. Maybe at first glance the seat looked good; it may have even felt good—nice leather, a cool shade of blue. But when you actually sat in it or tried to sleep in it on your way to Buenos Aires, it turned out to be very uncomfortable. And it's obvious at that point that you don't have to have the word *design* in your title or wear cool shoes to make an astute value judgment about design.

Art vs. Design

So, if everyone is a designer, and everything is designed, how do you know when something is *really* good? It's simple enough to agree that if a seat on an airplane is uncomfortable it isn't good design, but how can you begin to use design to create real business value?

In so many cases, what seems good is in the eye of the beholder: Is one font really going to move product more than another? Is one shade of Google blue really going to be superior to others?

People often say things like, "You really have an eye for design." I never really know what that means. But it's what we've come to expect when the word *design* is used interchangeably with words like *art* or *creativity*. So, let's see if we can distinguish between these terms.

Every child is born knowing how to pick up a crayon and draw. Or, if given macaroni, glue, and glitter, they can make something you might even call *art*. Okay, if not art, you'd say your kid was certainly *creative*. Especially on parents' night at school, when you see your kid's macaroni masterpiece hanging next to the others you may have thought, *Yep, that's my kid's art—it's much better than that kid's art.*

Art is very subjective, even if you take the influence of parenthood out of it. As we get older or exposed to different forms, we begin to have an opinion about the kind of art we *like*. Our world view expands. Our taste moves beyond macaroni masterpieces to Monet or Mondrian.

But that is all it is—just our subjective opinion. In reality, the artist—the person who created the thing—generally doesn't really care about what you think. It's *his* self-expression, *his* point-of-view, *his* take on the subject matter at hand. If you like it, you buy it. If you don't, you won't. This is why some people say you can't really *understand* art—you just have to feel it or experience it.

But design is different.

---

*Design is about intentionally connecting things
to solve problems.*

Design is only *good* if it solves a problem. Good design makes something easier to read, easier to understand, easier to use. Good design makes a difficult task less complicated.

Thus, the design of a book is *the way* the concepts, the tone of voice, the character development, the fonts, the paper or screen, all combine or connect to convey the story, not simply the object itself. The design of your phone is *the way* it helps you do what you need to do with it— make a call, send a text—not just materials used or the shape of the hardware. Lots of elements have to connect when you push a button on your phone to make a call. It all comes together for you to let your spouse know you'll be late for dinner. The value lies in ease of use and helping you solve your problem, not just the object's form or beauty.

This is where we can really begin to start to understand the value of design, especially if you're in business. If you can use design to solve problems, especially big problems that lots of people have, then lots of people will want to buy what you make, work for your company, or invest in your stock. But there's more.

One of the chief concerns for all businesses is financial: How do you grow your top-line revenues and/or reduce your bottom-line operating expenses? Those numbers at the bottom of a balance sheet are not very subjective, and have nothing to do with self- expression. In fact, in business, abstract, conceptual things are mostly rejected in a search for clarity that will ultimately help drive profitable growth for the company.

If you want to run a company successfully, you have to solve problems for your firm, your customers, or your stakeholders. This has everything to do with design and almost nothing to do with art. As a business, you may use art to stimulate. But you need design to solve problems.

Good design solves problems in a way that feels simpler, easier, better—in short, less complicated. Bad design may solve one problem, but create another in the process. At its worst, it can make even simple things more difficult.

Good design makes things less complicated.
Bad design makes things more complicated.

A classic example is the TV remote. I used to have a remote that made me feel bad every time I used it. At first I thought it was me, that I just wasn't smart enough to figure it out. Then I read the directions carefully, and tried hard to use it again. Couldn't do it. Bad design like that is all around us. We've come to expect it.

One of my favorite graphic designers, Paul Rand, put it this way: "The public is more familiar with bad design than good design. It is, in effect, conditioned to prefer bad design, because that is what it lives with."

Bad design is the default mode, since it takes the least effort to create.

Good design, by contrast, never happens by chance—you have to be very intentional.

Once you understand that we're all designers and the difference between good and bad design, we need to go one more level down; we need also to understand how design relates to the stuff that we can't see.

To really understand the value of design, you have to begin to understand how the visible and the invisible elements connect.

For example, remember the last time you were in the market for a new apartment or house. You weren't just looking for great doorknobs or a beautiful carpet. You didn't buy the house because of the curve in the driveway. The decision was also based on the price, your commute to the office, the crime rate of the neighborhood, the potential resale value, the neighbors, and the schools. Some of what you evaluated was easy to see. Other things were invisible—not immediately apparent, but just as important.

Of course you looked at everything individually, but you were looking for the total package or the end-to-end solution to your problem of finding a new place to live. In the end, what prompted you to rent or buy the place was how all of these individual things added up. All of the places you looked at probably had the same basic elements but the one you picked was likely the one where all of the pieces added up to feel very *connected*—everything worked together in a way that made it seem like a better *value* than the others. And that's how design creates the most value for companies—by connecting things seamlessly, intuitively, and appealingly.

But how does this all work? How can you use design to connect the stuff you can see with the stuff you can't see?

Systems and Design

Another way to think about how visible and invisible elements connect is to think about them as a system. There are many ways to define a *system*, but I like the way Donella Meadows, one of the foremost experts in systems theory, defines it: as "a set of things—people, cells, molecules, or whatever—interconnected in such a way that they produce their own pattern of behavior over time."

The way I can easily remember the definition is . . .

A system is a set of elements and behaviors that connect to do one thing.

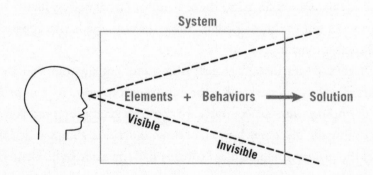

Most of the time the elements are easy to see—the tangible stuff—a door handle, a button, a product's packaging, and so on. But it's harder to see behaviors. Behaviors are how the various elements work together to do something.

If you're in business, your goal is to make sure the visible stuff (your products, your communications, your employees, etc.) connects to the invisible stuff (your partnerships, your processes, your culture) in a way that helps your company succeed. If they don't connect in the right way, this can actually hinder growth. And this is how design becomes *strategic*—in other words, the way you design, or the way you connect the visible with the invisible can actually enable growth or prevent it.

For example, what makes one soccer team better than another? On the surface, they all basically look the same. They have the same number of players, same basic uniform, same kinds of shoes, same kind of ball, and so forth. But a winning soccer team is about much more than those things.

Everybody knows the way the players behave and connect with each other on the field is what creates the power. Each team has a specific *way* in which they play to win. So, when you watch a team like Spain's Real Madrid or Germany's Bayern München, you marvel not only at what you see but also what you don't see. As a team, they are *designed* to win.

As a company, that's the challenge: to design elements like logos, products, supply chains, and so on, so that they work together to create growth for the company.

Let's contrast our soccer example with a system that wasn't designed very well.

In the United States, President Obama chose universal healthcare as the signature piece of legislation of his presidency. Giving everyone access to affordable healthcare is a very big and complex problem—needing a holistic, end-to-end solution.

However, in late 2013, when the program was launched, it was clear that there was a big problem—a design problem. A lot of people focused on what was visible, easy to see—the Web site—www.healthcare.gov. Trying to register on the site or search for a service provider was very complicated. Many people complained of waiting interminably before being redirected to an error page that said something like, "Error from: https%3A//www.healthcare.gov/oberr.cgi%3Fstatus%253D500%252 0errmsg%253DErrEngineDown%23signUpStepOne."

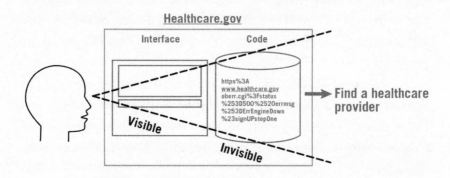

However, what many people didn't realize was that the front-end interface was designed by one company and the back end, the server-side code which handled all of the various processes (registration, search, etc.), was designed by a different firm. The user-interface is the part of Healthcare.gov that everyone can see—the *elements* like the buttons and photographs. And the back end—the code—was the part that no one could see. It drove the *behaviors* associated with finding a provider. Each was designed in a silo and didn't connect. Whoever managed the design process didn't think about all of the elements and behaviors as a system. They didn't *intentionally connect all of the elements and behaviors to solve a problem.*

Once the problems became apparent, the team moved to fix the troubled site by getting everybody on the same page. By December, they reported that the site "worked smoothly for the vast majority of users." Things had finally begun to connect—the back end to the front end to the people who logged on to use it.

All too often, problems don't exist in isolation. You can't solve one without affecting another. This is where design creates value that's hard to see or quantify, in that, by connecting things more smoothly, the entire experience improves.

Professional designers do this for a living. They are expert connectors. They know how to connect that bridge to the highway to the airport. And, once inside, they know how to connect the kiosks to the security lines to the seats at the gate. They understand how all of those things connect to the flight patterns of the airlines to the cities, highways, and bridges at the other end.

They're the ones responsible for connecting the user interface on your Web site to the billing system to the warehouse to the boxes and bubble wrap for the product you're selling. You don't have to be a professional designer to know when things are well connected; everything just feels less complicated. And, if they're not connecting well, problems invariably result: bad highway design leads to traffic jams, bad Web site design means users bail before purchasing, and bad security design means missed flights.

Anyone can learn how to connect things in a way that makes them less complicated, simpler, and easier to do. Connecting can apply both to very tangible things like machines to abstract things like supply chains, organization charts, and customer relationships.

When you design the solution as a system, you can begin to solve many connected problems, across your business.

So, to see how this works in practice, let's head back to Japan, where the Coca-Cola team is trying to fix its troubled bottled water business.

Redesigning Minaqua

With Minaqua there wasn't just one issue, there were many. Not only was each of these business problems challenging on its own, but they were all the more complex because they were also connected. Addressing just one of them wasn't going to turn the business around. Somehow, they all needed to be solved simultaneously.

But, where to begin? In short, how do you begin to redesign *everything*, at the *same time*?

Selling water is different from selling smartphones. You can't just redesign the shape of the product or add a new feature like retina display to gain market share. The Minaqua team knew that it would need to design new advertising, maybe a new Web site, probably a new package. It also knew it needed to look at the product's pricing strategy, customer relationships, and supply chain. It knew there had to be synergy among all of these to get the business growing again.

A small crossfunctional, multidisciplined team was assembled in Tokyo. It included designers, strategic planners, marketers, engineers, brand managers, customer relationship managers, and guys from the bottling operation who were experts on manufacturing and logistics. They uncovered a key insight: In Japan, recycling is not a nice-to-have; it's a way of life. Japan recycles more than 70 percent of its plastics and more than 80 percent of aluminum cans. (Compare that to the United States, which recycles a disappointing 31.5 percent of its waste.) When the team stepped back and looked at Minaqua, it was clear that the product wasn't connecting to any of this insight.

If the team could tap into that national commitment to responsible behavior, and redesign the whole water brand around this insight, it might be able to reverse the decline of the company's water business.

One other bit of data caught the team's attention. Tokyo alone is home to 13 million people. While the city no longer ranks as the largest in the world, its vast, 800 square mile metropolitan area gives it bragging rights as the world's largest, with 20 million people—26.5 million if you add in neighboring Yokohama. It's also an expensive place to live, often topping lists of the world's priciest cities.

That means housing prices are steep, especially around the center of the city, and the average size of an apartment is small. *The New York Times* reported that a typical unit runs about 70 square meters, or 750 square feet. Compare that to the United States, with an average of 214 square meters, or Australia with 206.

Why would the Minaqua team care about housing sizes in Tokyo? Simple: a bin of empty water bottles takes up valuable space. That might not be a big deal in a garage in suburban Chicago, but in a place where every square inch is precious, the volume of solid waste matters.

The problems were clear: slipping sales, undifferentiated product, challenges around packaging. And so was the opportunity: a country's passion for recycling, and an eagerness to do the right thing in the face of some serious hurdles.

In 2009, Coca-Cola Japan introduced an all new Japanese brand of water, ILOHAS (Lifestyles of Health and Sustainability). It came packaged in a new Flex bottle, which weighed just 12 grams when it was empty, 40 percent less than the company's other plastic bottles and the lightest package in Japan. Using a bottle that light allowed the company to reduce the amount of carbon dioxide produced in the manufacturing process by an estimated 3,000 tons. That's equivalent to a 24,000 acre forest. It also meant lighter delivery loads, recycling shipments with less wasted air, and a smaller number of waste disposal emissions. The company was designing on purpose: connecting things across the entire system—from less plastic in manufacturing (resulting in cost savings) to a smaller carbon footprint (less impact on the planet).

However, that wasn't the fun part. Because the bottle is so light, it can easily be twisted by hand into a thin, gnarly scrap of plastic. That means it takes up significantly less room in recycling bins. What's more, it makes a delicious crunching sound when you twist it. The pleasure is almost as intense as when you pop the pods in a sheet of bubble wrap. Plus, that let the team get around another problem it discovered: Women don't like to crush bottles with their shoes. It's nasty getting a squished water bottle stuck on the heel of your Jimmy Choo stilettos!

The team in Japan designed an advertising campaign that connected the message that ILOHAS is the "water which changes the world with your small action" with the design of a new ritual that reinforced the brand message. The ritual itself was simple : 1. Choose, 2. Drink, 3. Twist, 4. Recycle.

That simple message went viral in Japan, where consumers posted videos on YouTube featuring themselves twisting and art students created films using the cast-offs. What's more, sales of the product spiked by double digits in fewer than six months, along with a dramatic rise in recycling, despite our charging a premium price for the brand.

The critical thing to note is that no one thing was more important than the other; success came from how each element was designed to work with all the others.

So, where do *you* begin? What does this mean for your team, your function, or your company? How can you ensure that you're designing in a way that helps you win? One way is by making sure that you're clear about *why* you're doing what you're doing, before you start figuring out *how* to do it. A famous TED talk explains how this works.

Designing for the *Why*

Have you ever heard of the Golden Circle? It's a model that Simon Sinek, researcher, author, and educator, first introduced in his book, *Start With Why,* and elaborated on in a TED talk in 2009.

Sinek uses a simple model—three concentric circles—to discuss the interdependencies between the what, how, and why great people and companies succeed. Great leaders, companies, or individuals "think, act, and communicate" and "inspire action" by starting with the *Why*. They focus on their purpose first—why they do what they do—not *how* they do it or *what* they make. As you'd imagine, he's a great communicator—once you watch the video, it's hard to get his mantra that "people don't buy what you do, they buy *why* you do it" out of your head.

When I first saw the talk, I was blown away with Sinek's ability to make such a complicated concept easy to understand. After I watched it a few more times, I remember scribbling the circles on a Post-it note and adding the word *design* to the framework.

The Golden Circle

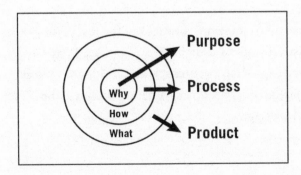

By the time I first encountered Sinek, we had been working for almost five years to transform the way we designed—the "How" we designed. We also had the idea, spelled out in my Jerry Maguire manifesto, that we should always be "designing on purpose," starting with the *Why*. Most of the projects that we'll discuss in Part 2, such as the Freestyle drink machine; the marketing tool Design Machine; and the 5-Note Melody were in full development.

Once I simply added the word *design* to Sinek's model, something clicked—everything connected—the interdependencies between the *Why, How,* and *What* of design. I started using Sinek's model to talk about design.

Now, there's no *magic* in the Golden Circle model. It was just another tool we've used to help everyone understand design and ultimately create more value. However, Sinek's model helped me to understand what often is missing as companies grapple with the place of design in their organizations.

---

*Most companies focus on what they design.
Companies that get the full value out of design
start with why they design and then shape how
they design—their process—around their purpose.*

We'll use this framework throughout the rest of the book to help us think holistically about design. *Why* becomes, Why we design—our *purpose* for design. *How* becomes, How we design—our *process* for design. And lastly, *What* becomes, What we design—the *type* of product or service we design.

LESSON LEARNED #2

Are you thinking about design holistically?

Ask yourself these three questions:

1. Is design aligned with your growth strategy?

Start with the *Why*—what's the purpose driving how you design in your organization? Is your growth strategy more about growing through scale or agility?

2. What's your design process?

Then move to the *how*—what's your design process? Have you codified how your organization designs? Does it align with your growth strategy—your *Why*? If so, how consistent is your approach across the organization?

3. Do your products (or services) enable your Why?

Does everything connect to enable your purpose? Does the invisible connect with the visible? When you look at your products or services—are all of the elements and behaviors connected to drive the *Why*?

Thinking holistically about design—the *Why, How,* and *What*—can create competitive advantage and growth for anyone. But how does that simple idea translate into a company that operates in over 200 countries with billion-dollar brands? Understanding the power of design is one thing, but creating that kind of value is rare.

For a century, The Coca-Cola Company channeled the power of design to strategically grow its business by designing for scale. But as we've seen with the ILOHAS example, it takes more than scale to win in today's world. Today, we must design in a way that's agile enough to adapt to a vast array of different environments and needs.

Most companies that operate successfully on a global scale have figured that out. That's why you can get McBaguettes in McDonald's in France, and McAloo Tikki potato burgers at McDonald's in India. But Minaqua, the example that opened this chapter, demonstrates the need to ramp this capability up one more level. In a complex world, it's also not enough simply to put a product out there in a range of variations and through a variety of channels and hope for the best.

We need to think bigger. We need to think about resource scarcity—in the case of ILOHAS, the plastic (PET) used for the bottle and how to minimize the amount used. We need to think about the *Why*—the context—in this case, the space constraints of Japanese apartments that make having a recycling bin of empty bottles in the kitchen impractical. We need to think about culture—in Tokyo, the Japanese ethos around sustainability. We need to think about social media—with ILOHAS, how designing a ritual around recycling had the potential to inspire behavior if it caught on. In short, the company needed to think about the entirety of the product, from its birth to its afterlife, in order to design it in a way that creates the most competitive advantage, while simultaneously creating shared value for partners, whether they are retailers of the beverage, package recyclers, or consumers who simply wanted to dispose of a container responsibly after using it.

In our next chapter, we'll go a step deeper and dig into how design can create scale. We'll show how The Coca-Cola Company used design, very strategically, to scale from a little startup to a billion-dollar, multinational company.

CHAPTER 2

Scale

What's great about this country is that America started the
tradition where the richest consumers buy essentially the
same things as the poorest. You can be watching TV and see
Coca-Cola, and you know that the President drinks Coca-
Cola, Liz Taylor drinks Coca-Cola, and just think, you can
drink Coca-Cola, too. A Coke is a Coke and no amount of
money can get you a better Coke than the one the bum on
the corner is drinking. All the Cokes are the same and all the
Cokes are good. Liz Taylor knows it, the President knows it,
the bum knows it, and you know it.

Andy Warhol

What makes a company great? Superior products, certainly. A corporate culture that rewards excellence and discipline, led by a
humble CEO, according to Jim Collins, who wrote the seminal book
on the topic, *Good to Great*. But many of the companies that Collins
identified haven't done too well in recent years, despite hitting the
mark on the measures he identified.

The traits that seem to separate the winners from the also-rans in
today's highly volatile marketplace are the ability to grow a business
while keeping its essential value proposition intact, that is, to scale,

and the talent for adapting to meet the ever-changing demands of the marketplace—a knack for agility.

When The Coca-Cola Company was founded in 1886, it was like many of today's startups: Its founder had the drive to succeed, little money, and lots of business problems. But, over the course of its history, the company was also blessed with leaders who showed a prescient understanding of the market, a willingness to take risks, and a remarkable dexterity for changing with the time, what we would now call a *willingness to pivot*.

Let's take a brief spin through Coca-Cola's history to see just what decisions fueled its growth from one man's big idea into a multibillion dollar company.

The founder of Coca-Cola, John Pemberton, was a trained pharmacist with a bushy beard and the formula for a new secret concoction. He came to Atlanta, Georgia, in 1869, just four years after the end of the American Civil War. A wounded veteran, Pemberton was looking for a fresh start. Like every entrepreneur, he had the germ of an idea and wanted to start his own business. Short on cash, he moved into a boarding house, where he lived and worked with other entrepreneurs who were also trying to get their ideas off the ground—an early version of a co-working space.

Before long, he launched the Pemberton Chemical Company and began raising his first round of seed funding.

At the time, the market for new beverages was exploding. These were the apps of their day. New products like sarsaparilla, Dr. Pepper, and many others were fueling a fast growing market. Pemberton was hoping for his own "unicorn." If he could develop something a little different, he was sure he could succeed.

Over the next few years, he rolled out six new products. All of them failed. He just couldn't find the right product/market fit.

Then, things changed. He stirred up a cola-flavored syrup in a brass kettle, mixed it with soda water, and got a warm reception from a small group of beverage enthusiasts at a popular soda fountain in Atlanta.

In 1886, he got his investors together for a quick demo day and pitched his new product. They loved it and decided to back him with more funding. That was the first hurdle. However, Pemberton knew that he needed more than just a product to compete in the frenzied beverage marketplace of the 1880s. He needed to make his product stand out from the others; he needed to create a powerful brand.

Pemberton's investors were eager to help. Frank Robinson, the new company's accountant, was partial to alliteration, which was in vogue at the time. He suggested calling the new concoction "Coca-Cola," and wrote out the logo in his own lyrical script. It was the birth of what would become one of the world's biggest brands.

Like most founders, Pemberton struggled with scale.

Pemberton's first year's revenues were fifty dollars; his expenses, seventy-six dollars. By the second year, things weren't looking any better. He was running out of money and his health was not good.

In 1888, Asa Candler, the founder of three other companies, met with Pemberton and offered to buy his company for $2,300. Pemberton got the exit he needed and Candler began selling Coca-Cola. It took almost three years of bootstrapping and iterating, but Candler finally found the business model that worked. He renamed the company, "The Coca-Cola Company" and began to add staff and enlarge the company's operations. Over the next ten years, Candler and the company's fifty employees scaled Coca-Cola into a million-dollar national brand, expanding to every state in the United States.

In 1899, Candler made another change in the company's business model. It might have been the pivot of the century. Two young entrepreneurs from Tennessee, Benjamin Franklin Thomas and Joseph

Whitehead, pitched Candler an idea: They wanted to start a new company that would make it easier for people to drink Coca-Cola on the go. Candler was skeptical, but eventually sold them the rights to bottle and sell Coca-Cola for just one dollar.

Much to Candler's surprise, it worked. He quickly adopted a franchise business model and built a network of hundreds of independent bottlers. In the process, he launched not only a high-growth company, but a new industry. Candler was the Henry Ford of the soft drink industry.

In 1919, a group of investors bought The Coca-Cola Company for $25 million. They reincorporated the company and took it public, selling 500,000 shares of common stock for forty dollars per share—the biggest IPO of its day in the food and beverage industry. Four years later, Robert Woodruff was elected president of the company. The thirty-three-year-old president would spend the next six decades putting Coca-Cola "within arm's reach of desire," creating one of the most valuable brands in the world.

In this chapter, we're going to show how The Coca-Cola Company strategically used design to scale from a little startup to a billion-dollar, multinational company.

Designing for Scale

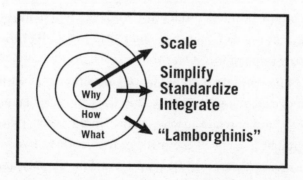

Using the approach inspired by Sinek's model, the *Why* or purpose of design in this case is *scale*. The *How*, or process, is to *simplify, standardize,* and *integrate.* And the *What*, or product we'll be designing, are Lamborghinis.

Okay, I know you thought we were discussing a beverage company here, but stick with me and eventually it will all make sense. Before we figure out how to scale the design of fancy sports cars, let's explore what scale means in a more common situation—a few founders in an early stage startup trying to launch a new app-based business.

Scale

Let's begin with a simple definition of scale:

---

*Scale is the ability to increase in quantity
without reducing quality or profit.*

All companies struggle with scale on some dimension. Every company is trying to expand to the next level, however they may define it, but startups have an especially hard time. All startups are temporary. They only exist to find a viable business model. Their goal is to grow from this preliminary state into a great company. Let's imagine we're in a startup, to get a feel for how volatile life can be, and how difficult it is for them to scale.

For a lot of startups, their value proposition begins with an app. Apps allow early stage companies to scale very fast with few additional resources. So, let's say our product is an app that helps people find temporary jobs on demand.

We released the newest version of our app last Monday with a new feature we're testing. By week two, we see a huge spike in adoption. Our users double—amazing! On Thursday of that same week, a deal we'd been working on falls through—disaster! Without that deal, we can't expand into a new market. Without the deal, we can't compete with a new Brazilian startup that launched last month and has targeted our user base. We've heard they are very well funded and are moving fast. We all meet at the end of the day to figure out if we can stretch our seed funding and find another partner. But at the end of the meeting everyone is thinking, *game over—six months down the drain.*

On Saturday, we do a quick test with a potential new customer. We pitch an idea that perhaps would shift us to a B2B business model. By the following week, we decide to pivot and relaunch our new B2B model under a completely different name. Two weeks later, the big enterprise customer that we've been trying to land for months finally signs a contract. We're back on track, ready to change the world.

This type of flux can't go on forever. The startup either runs out of runway and dies—it can't hire the right team, blows through its funding, can't get the customers it needs, or any one of a dozen other problems. Or it makes it—it validates its business model and stabilizes. The startup begins to generate revenue, and its brand begins to build a reputation. At that point, it morphs from being a *startup* to being a *company* and focuses on scaling its operations, team, customer base, and processes.

The challenge for every startup is scale. Usually this means two things—scaling your product and scaling your business model. This sounds kind of simple. It isn't. Most startups die in the process. These are the questions startups need to answer if they are to become viable companies.

1. How can we create a product that can scale up and down?
    As sales grow, patterns begin to develop. Your challenge is to figure out how to make more stuff when your custom-

ers need it, and less when they don't (and do all of this at the same level of quality). If you can figure out how to scale your product up and down depending on demand, you can manage cash flow, build trust in your brand, insure consistency with your stakeholders, and, hopefully, attract loyal customers.

2. How can we create a business model that will scale?

The first question was about quality—this question is about quantity. If you're in a startup, it's infernally hard to find a product that a lot of people need inside a fast-growing industry. It's even harder to figure out how to make it, distribute it, and sell it for a profit. As we've noted earlier, only one out of ten startups makes it.

If you're one of them, your next step is to figure out how to *do more for the same cost.* If, for example, in year one, you generate $1M in revenue at an operating cost of $100,000, then your goal for year two should be to generate $2M in revenue at an operating cost of $100,000—to keep your costs flat while increasing your revenue. If it costs you $200,000 to generate $2M in revenue, your business model won't scale. Back to the whiteboard.

LESSON LEARNED #3

Go for Buy-in, Not Credit

Everybody likes to be recognized for a job well done. It's human nature. But I've discovered that there's one thing more important than making a name for yourself if you really want to create change. It's getting buy-in—

getting everyone in the company to *want* to move in the same direction. A big part of getting buy-in is not worrying about getting credit personally when something goes well (or worrying about taking the heat when something doesn't).

Almost every time I'm asked to do a talk, someone asks me a question about getting buy-in. The questions are always phrased differently, but they go something like, "How were you able to get different teams to work together on that project?" Or "How can we get our senior management to focus on innovation?"

The first thing out of my mouth is always the same: "Remember, it's never about you." It will never work if you're trying to somehow leverage the company, the brands, or the people you work with to make a big name for yourself. People can see that a mile away. And, no matter how often you speak, how many followers you have on Twitter, or how many magazine covers you're on, you'll never get real change if you focus primarily on yourself, ensuring that all praise and honor circles back to you or your team.

In 2009, *Fast Company* recognized me in its annual Masters of Design issue. Of course, when I found out they were considering me I was very excited. Who wouldn't be? But, to be honest, I was also very afraid. When you do an interview for a magazine or some other kind of media, you never know what's going to happen—you can't control what they write.

By the time that opportunity rolled around, we had been building a design-driven culture for about five years—and had made significant progress—more than I could have imagined when I started. We had a lot to talk about—lots of proof points—lots of buy-in. The last thing I wanted to do was derail all of this, lose trust, and somehow betray the company by making the whole thing appear to be about me.

When the reporter came to Atlanta to interview me, I urged her to speak to a variety of people—not just our small design team but many other people at different levels and locations of the company. It was really important to get a holistic view of design at the company because what we were doing with design could only happen if everyone *wanted* to move in the same direction. We had moved design to a way of thinking, not just doing.

When the issue came out, there was a little bit of tension in the beginning (after all, it was still *my* face on the cover), but for the most part everyone saw the piece as recognition for the company, not David Butler. Most people were proud that The Coca-Cola Company had been recognized as being design-driven. And that's exactly what I was hoping for.

Key Takeaway: It's never about me—it's always about we.

Simplify, Standardize, Integrate

If we think back to the golden circle, *scale is our Why—our purpose. How we design* and *What we design* must be driven by our growth strategy based on scale.

When startups reach the point at which they shift their purpose from survival to scale, it feels very different. Up until then, the name of the game is simply to stay alive—to do whatever it takes to make it to the next milestone. There are no end-to-end processes, no employee handbooks, barely any structure, and few, if any, rules. Now, they need some. To have any chance of scaling, they need to figure out what is working, and do it much more consistently, whether it's packing boxes, hiring developers, or processing travel and expense reports.

To begin to scale, they need to figure out a way to keep their operating costs fixed, and increase their revenue while maintaining a consistent level of quality. This is where design comes in.

Scale is all about flawless execution—to create or leverage scale, everything must be designed to make it as easy as possible to execute with precision. To do this, you must eliminate all ambiguity, excess, and waste.

To achieve scale, everything must be simplified and standardized to integrate with the least amount of friction.

Your goal is to create a *perfect* solution—in this case, imagine a Lamborghini—that can then be standardized and mass produced. A Lamborghini is designed to be perfect. Each piece is handcrafted to work specifically with the other pieces exclusively with little to no friction, as an integrated system. There's not a lot of mixing and matching going on inside the factory in Sant'Agata. Each individual piece must be purposely designed to do one unique thing, and that piece must connect perfectly with the other pieces. There are no more iterations or pivots. Experimentation is over. This is all about execution and perfection. This is the only way to keep your operating costs fixed and to maintain a consistent level of quality.

This is very different from what you've been doing as a startup. In the beginning, it's all about speed and constant experimentation. Creating a product that people need and finding a business model that generates revenue is hard enough. Now you need to generate a lot more revenue while keeping your operating costs the same. This is the point at which you can leverage the power of design.

Up to now, you've been designing a kit car—bolting on things as they make sense—just to keep the car running. Now it's time to transform your kit car into a precision automobile by simplifying and standardizing everything that makes your business model work. All those elements of the product and organization must connect with as much effectiveness and efficiency as possible. Everything must now be designed on purpose.

You must understand what makes people love your product or service more than your competitor's, and the nuances around what makes your product or brand unique. Then, you need to create a passion for those details to make sure everyone in your company understands how important it is to get them right every time.

When a company gets the details right, you don't have to be a designer to know a product is good—it just *feels* right. When companies are able to do this at national or global scale, their products often become iconic or classics—symbolic of the highest level of quality in their category. Chanel's No. 5 Parfum, a Porsche 911, and the Eames Lounge Chair are all products that manage to cross cultures and geographies and rise above their peers to symbolize the best of the best.

Most of the time, great design means getting the details right.

The stitching on a handbag, the sound of an engine, the placement of a button on an app. When every detail is considered, the whole experience feels good. None of this happens by accident; everything must be designed to work that way.

Charles Eames himself once said, "The details are not the details. They *make* the design. . . . Eventually everything connects—people, ideas, objects. The quality of the connections is the key to quality per se."

If you own an Eames Lounge Chair, you know exactly what he meant. Today's version has been essentially unchanged since 1956. Its two curved forms interlock in a way that is unmistakable and difficult to copy. However, it's not just the way it looks that makes it unique. It's one of the most comfortable chairs in the world. These are the details that, together, make it a classic.

The secret behind such iconic products from Louisville Slugger bats, to even Amazon's 1-Click Ordering, is that the company behind them has designed these products in a way that these details don't change. They are locked down, held sacred and secure. As these companies have scaled over time, including manufacturing and distribution all over the world, every element remains consistent. You can buy a Porsche 911 in Beijing or Boston, and it will be essentially the same.

That's the key: You must understand the critical details that make your product unique—the specific things that people love—and then codify them so that they remain fixed over time and across geographies.

Once you do this, it's time to standardize as much as possible. Standardization helps a company plan, resource, predict, and ultimately, grow consistently. Everyone moves in the same direction. That creates massive efficiency. But how does this work?

Standards create a common language and clear direction.

Standards are all about reduction. They make big problems easier by taking the decision making out of the process and replacing it with a few easy-to-follow steps. This is really helpful when a company begins to add a lot of products, people, cultures, currencies, regulations, languages, and so on. Standards create a common language for everybody in the company.

Nobody does this better than Walmart, the world's largest retailer.

According to *Fortune,* the company sold $421,849B worth of stuff in 2011. If Walmart were a country, it would be the twenty-fifth largest economy in the world.

How is this possible?

It all comes down to boxes.

From the cardboard box containing its products to the big box of its retail stores, Walmart manages everything by designing boxes. Cardboard box sizes are designed not only to consolidate packaging and minimize space requirements, but to fit on pallets, forklifts, conveyer belts, and robots. Each box is managed through RFID (Radio Frequency Identification).

Those boxes are designed to fix in an even bigger box, the shipping container which, in the 1960s, established the twenty-foot equivalent unit (TEU). That measurement essentially standardized the consumer goods industry globally. Entire fleets and harbors had to be rebuilt to align with this standard.

And it doesn't stop there: Walmart's big-box store formats are designed to a standard formula, walmart.com is designed using pixels (little boxes), and on and on. This is how big companies manage global scale, by reducing the scale of the earth by thinking small.

So, how do you design standards? It all comes down to two things: The first one is easy to understand, but difficult to do.

Think small.

The challenge is to simplify, simplify, and simplify, until you get to the fewest number of elements, which become your common denominators. For Walmart, reducing to a system of boxes helps maintain its gold standard around execution and logistics. This design strategy can apply to almost anything.

About a year after I came to the company, my team and I did a global audit to try to understand the state of Coca-Cola's brand identity around the world. We soon realized that we had a big challenge on our hands. There wasn't a clear, strategic direction or common system for the brand's visual identity from market to market.

We knew what we had to do. We went back to the archives, and looked for patterns that worked in the past. We knew we needed to find the details that made Coca-Cola *Coca-Cola*, then simplify and standardize.

One of our design directors and I sought out examples of what Coke looked like when everyone felt it was most authentic. Once we saw the power and simplicity of the original red and white label design from the 1970s, our task was obvious: to go back to the basics of the brand's essence, so that the strength of the Coca-Cola brand was clear.

We stripped away everything that wasn't authentic to the brand. When we were finished, a lot of people said that we had gone retro. It was a fair criticism, but missed the point. We were striving not only for authenticity, but global consistency. We wanted to make it easy for everyone in our company to *revive the icon*, a shorthand phrase which came to symbolize the new brand strategy.

It wasn't as easy as it sounds, but it worked.

That brings us to the second thing you must do when designing standards.

Make it easy to do the right thing.

You must create a tool that makes it easy for everyone in your company to execute according to standard. This might be an email, a brochure, or a Web site. We created an internal web-based tool, the Design

Machine, which archives all the elements of all of our brand identity systems. That tool allows anyone to create any piece of communication, from point of purchase displays, to packaging, to coolers, to banner advertising, independently, efficiently, and in total alignment with our standards. We'll discuss this further in chapter 6.

The goal, in developing standards, is to create a *perfect* solution—a Lamborghini, a Stradivarius—that can then be mass produced. Each individual piece must be designed to do one unique thing, and that piece must connect with all the other pieces, seamlessly, intuitively, perfectly. You have to think of the end result as a masterpiece, whether your product is as simple as a bottle of dish soap or as complicated as a new way to stream music.

LESSON LEARNED #4

Identify Patterns

One of my favorite books is *A Pattern Language* by Christopher Alexander, Sara Ishikawa, and Murray Silverstein. Originally published in 1977, the book is a classic—a textbook for most first-year architects.

The book introduces the concept of using patterns to design cities, buildings, houses, and rooms. It's based on the concept that all great homes and metropolises feel *alive*. What makes them feel this way is a set of patterns that can be applied by anyone.

"Each pattern describes a problem which occurs over and over again in our environment, and then describes the core of the solution to that problem in such a way that you can use this solution a million times over, without ever doing it the same way twice."

For example, Pattern 167, Six-Foot Balcony, describes the fundamentals you need to construct a balcony. It's very practical, easy to understand and apply. The pattern is that balconies and porches need to be at least six feet deep—enough that two people can sit comfortably around a small side table. If a balcony is smaller than that, which sometimes happens when builders try to save money, it will hardly ever be used.

These patterns, the authors stress, need to be viewed holistically.

"No pattern is an isolated entity. Each pattern can exist in the world, only to the extent that is supported by other patterns: the larger patterns in which it is embedded, the patterns of the same size that surround it, and the smaller patterns which are embedded in it."

Imagine an apartment building. Each of the balconies, on each of the floors, must be the same size. Differing sizes would destroy the building's symmetry, but within each balcony, the spaces between the bars on the railing, or the tiles on the floor, form their own patterns.

"This is a fundamental view of the world. It says that when you build a thing you cannot merely build that thing in isolation, but must also repair the world around it, and within it, so that the larger world at the one place becomes more coherent, and more whole; and the thing which you make takes its place in the web of nature, as you make it."

In other words, you can't put a Manhattan skyscraper in the middle of a village in Tuscany, or a Tuscan villa on Madison Avenue.

This way of using patterns can work for companies just as well as they work for homeowners and city planners. Once you identify the patterns, then your task is to get everyone to use them—and this is critical to scaling.

Another way to think about designing for scale is to find the patterns that have worked in the past or promising new ones, and then make them as easy as possible for everyone to repeat. That's typically called standardization.

Finding a winning pattern for your business involves

trial and error. Amazon tried a few things before hitting on 1-Click Ordering and Amazon Prime pricing for shipping, two things that have been instrumental in fueling the company's growth.

Diane von Furstenberg created her signature wrap dress in the 1970s when, newly divorced, she wanted a dress for herself that was simultaneously comfortable, powerful, and sexy. The fact that it looked good on a wide variety of women helped make it iconic.

> *Twitter's 140 characters, TED Talks' 18-minute rule, and TripAdvisor's rating system are all examples of patterns that companies have discovered work for them.*

While most of us don't think about it, somebody has to design a pattern in the first place. When they're right, they create speed, predictability, consistency, and simplicity. Patterns make it easier to do the right thing. If you're a company, that's the stuff that makes employees, investors, and Wall Street happy.

Designing patterns is another way to think about designing for scale. You have to get the details right, simplify, and standardize, then execute.

Scaling Coca-Cola

Over the years, I've tried to learn everything I could about the way Coca-Cola designed for scale. One day, as I was combing through the archives, I turned up a terrific photograph that perfectly illustrates the power of standardization. It's a picture from 1927 of two guys selling Coke out of a kiosk in Shanghai.

Imagine these two at the time—starting their own business with this new American product, Coca-Cola. Their kiosk is branded with signs that feature the now familiar contour glass bottle, the Coca-Coca logo against Coca-Cola red, with the message, "Sold Here. Ice Cold." What these guys didn't know was that there were entrepreneurs like them using the same product, logo, bottle, signage, and so on, all around the world. This is how the company was able to scale to twenty-eight countries by 1929.

In fact, there are seven different systems the company has used to scale Coca-Cola. Each of them was designed for scale and contributed to helping the company reach Robert Woodruff's vision to be "within arm's reach of desire."

1. The Formula

The concoction that John Pemberton brought to Atlanta in 1869 wasn't all that unusual. The market was flooded with new beverages, which were typically dispensed at soda fountains, cheery places where people liked to hang out.

In the early spring of 1886, in an attempt at marketing research, Pemberton sent his nephew, Lewis Newman, with samples of his concoctions to Venable's fountain at Jacob's Pharmacy in Atlanta, instructing him to hang around long enough to hear how patrons liked the new brews.

By the end of the year, he finally came up with a formula that people liked. He and his investors settled on a name, and a new company was born.

Very little has changed in the Coca-Cola pattern since it was launched over one hundred years ago. The formula, locked in a vault in Atlanta, is still the basis of the product. That has made it much easier for the company to scale into so many markets. Today, you can go almost anywhere in the world and find the familiar taste of Coca-Cola.

2. The Spencerian Script

As an accountant, Robinson was trained in writing Spencerian script, the standard handwriting method favored by double-entry bookkeepers in the 1880s. He thought that using a cursive form of the brand name would differentiate Coca-Cola from other brands. The company eventually standardized the logo in 1923, and it's exactly the same today, ninety years later. It is one of the most recognizable logos in the world.

Like any other company with a brand as valuable as Coca-Cola, the company has very detailed brand standards that make it easy for everyone to use the Spencerian script the way Coca-Cola would like them to. These standards are critical when it comes to execution.

3. The Contour Bottle

In the 1980 film *The Gods Must Be Crazy,* a tribe of Bushmen in the Kalahari Desert discover a glass Coca-Cola bottle that has fallen, unbroken, from an airplane. They think it's a wonderful artifact—a gift from the gods! The premise of the joke is that only a band of natives, on the fringes of civilization, wouldn't immediately recognize the world's most famous bottle.

The story of that iconic shape is actually a tale of defensive marketing, an attempt to distinguish a fledging brand after Candler's massive and successful marketing campaign had launched a thousand imitators.

The bottlers were eager to distinguish their product from the tide of copycats. Seeing competitors encroaching on his market, Thomas, the Chattanooga lawyer who had bought bottling rights for one dollar, told an associate, "We need a bottle which a person can recognize as a Coca-Cola bottle when he feels it in the dark ... so shaped that, even if broken, a person could tell at a glance what it was."

At the time, Coca-Cola's bottle, like most bottles for soda and beer, were simple things—straight-sided affairs with paper labels that were easy to duplicate. So, in 1915, in partnership with the bottlers, the company launched a contest for the design of a bottle that would be harder for imitators to knock off.

The design had to fit the existing bottling equipment so it could scale across the business. The winner stood to gain millions in royalties.

Casting about for inspiration, the folks at the Root Glass Company of Terre Haute, Indiana, seized on the word *Coca* in the drink's name. Combing through reference books for information under *coca* and *kola* didn't yield much, but under the entry for *cocoa*, the company's mold shop supervisor, Earl R. Dean, came upon an illustration that formed the seed of an idea.

"The pod was the size of a cucumber," Dean recalled in a 1971 interview, six months before he died, "with convolutions all around like a cantaloupe. It had a pinch in the middle, and a stem at the top like a squash." Ignoring the fact that Coca-Cola contained neither chocolate nor cocoa, Dean made a few drawings of what he saw.

Dean and the plant supervisor, Alexander Samuelson, labored for twenty-two hours straight to turn the cocoa-pod drawings into a three-dimensional object. Fifteen minutes before the factory shut down for annual maintenance, a few bottles were turned out.

At the bottlers' convention in 1916, the Root bottle was declared the winner, and was on shelves later that year. By

1920, *the contour bottle,* as it's been called, had become the company's most celebrated artifact.

That bottle has become one of the most recognized objects of the twentieth century, available in more than two hundred countries.

4. Thirty-Six Degrees

Coca-Cola was designed to be consumed at thirty-six degrees Fahrenheit (2.2 degrees Celsius). Internally, this standard is one of the elements of the "perfect serve"—the absolute best way to enjoy Coke. The carbonation, the formula, the glass bottle—all work best together at that temperature.

The thirty-six-degree standard was set along with the other standards during Woodruff's leadership. In the days before electric coolers, Coca-Cola salesmen would carry a thermometer designed to measure the temperature of the ice inside our customers' retail stores and kiosks. The ice-cold language the company used on its various pieces of point-of-sale communication (and gave to its retailers) was a subtle reminder that the company expected them to always serve Coca-Cola at no more than forty degrees.

5. The Nickel Price

For seventy years, from 1886 to after World War II, a bottle of Coca-Cola cost a nickel. The company and its bottling partners kept the price fixed through two World Wars, The Great Depression, sugar rationing, and a barrage of competition; it never varied.

The nickel price was part of a very innovative form of brand building as well. Candler and his team blanketed the country with giant ads, on the sides of buildings, barns, and billboards, trumpeting the five-cent price. For small business owners, these ads communicated progress—they, too, were part of this fast-growing brand that was taking off like a rocket.

Finally, in 1959, the company began raising its prices to better reflect its costs.

Keeping the price fixed for seven decades greatly simplified the business, and was critical in helping Coca-Cola scale globally.

6. Brand Marketing

By 1891, with the rights to Pemberton's chemical company in his back pocket, Candler conceived a prescient marketing ploy. Figuring that once people tried his new beverage they'd come back for more, he began showering the region with free-sample coupons.

He mailed little cards to area Chambers of Commerce and asked that the head of the organization distribute the coupons to the town's "most illustrious citizens." Coupons appeared in national magazine ads. Soda fountain operators were given a stack, along with a couple gallons of free syrup, and told to give the freebies to their most prominent patrons.

"Between 1887 and 1920, ten percent of all of our product was given away via sample coupons," says Ted Ryan, manager of Coca-Cola archives.

In the process, Candler had sketched the outlines for a strategy that would presage what we now call *word-of-mouth* or *influencer* marketing. And he laid the groundwork for what marketers at Coca-Cola now call *liquid marketing*, a way of marketing an idea across all platforms and media.

By 1895, Coca-Cola was being sold across the United States under the banner of a logo and name that everyone could recognize. That was Google-like growth for its time, and no other company could match its trajectory, its scale, or its consistency.

Candler didn't stop at couponing. He was a masterful brand marketer before anybody had ever heard of the idea. He began giving away a variety of promotional items: tip trays, calendars, glasses, clocks, pocket knives, paper fans, matchbooks, and playing cards all branded with the Coca-Cola name. It didn't matter that some of the items had nothing to do with a fountain beverage, as long as they featured Coca-Cola's brand identity.

Then, Candler took the messaging one step further. He designed a marketing campaign with a distinct look and feel. Posters, cutouts, and floral festoons were all provided free to proprietors of establishments that served his beverage, and were enhanced with pictures of pretty girls, all sipping Coke. Each picture had the same slogan, "Drink Coca-Cola. Delicious and refreshing."

Everywhere an ad for Coca-Cola appeared, it had the same four words. And soon, that message had a phenomenal national reach, with wall signs, ads painted on barns, newspaper advertising, and awnings all proclaiming the same thing. By 1908, some 2.5 million square feet of American building facades (and 10,000 more in Cuba and Canada) were advertising the delicious and refreshing properties of Coca-Cola, enhanced by its now ubiquitous script logo, and its consumer-friendly five-cent price. Designing for standardization helped scale the brand, and the company, on a national level.

7. The Franchise Business Model

Amid the soda wars that broke out in the 1880s, Candler's most significant business decision had nothing to do with branding.

Designing a business model that could scale required a different kind of thinking. What if, instead of selling the product in glasses in soda fountains, it was put in bottles to go?

In 1899, the two lawyers from Chattanooga, Tennessee, Thomas and Whitehead, struck a deal: one dollar for nearly all the United States rights.

Candler was no business rube. He understood that the arrangement that Thomas and Whitehead proposed had a certain irresistible genius. They could divide up the country, and sell a territory to a local entrepreneur who would put up the money for the glass and the trucks and the equipment to get the bottling business up and running. The two Tennesseans would buy the secret syrup from Coca-Cola, mark it up an eighth of a cent or so, and sell it to their local representatives. Those folks would bottle it, mark it up a couple of cents, and sell it off to eager customers for the very reasonable price of five cents.

"Everybody was only making a penny, but a penny on a billion servings is a lot of money," says Ryan.

This was the genesis of the company's franchise business model—what people internally call the Coca-Cola System—an interdependent partnership between The Coca-Cola Company and more than 250 independent bottling companies around the world.

The Coca-Cola bottlers, motivated by their own eagerness to build a business around a product that had an increasingly enthusiastic customer base and was supported by a robust national advertising campaign, enabled the business to grow exponentially. It proved to be a prescient decision, a way of designing for scale.

This model has allowed the company to leverage global brands but remain very local. And this is what drives its ability to execute. The Coca-Cola Company isn't one giant company; it's a system of small companies. And this pattern helps it scale new products, new communications, new equipment, etc. Designing for this pattern is critical; when it wants to scale fast, it can.

The Bureau of Standards

The company's passion for instituting standards reached its peak under Robert Woodruff, whose father led a group of investors that purchased the company for $25 million from Candler in 1919.

Woodruff came from the auto industry, having worked for the White Motor Car Company in Cleveland. While White was no Ford, it still followed the manufacturing principles of the day, which included a strict attention to standardization, as cars rolled off the conveyor belt.

Woodruff brought that mania for standardization to The Coca-Cola Company, issuing a series of guidebooks dictating the rules governing every aspect of the business. If you wanted to open a bottling plant, there was a set of instructions and blueprints on how to build the facility. If you wanted to paint a sign on the side of a barn, reminding passing motorists that Coca-Cola was delicious and refreshing, there was a sign-painting guide for that. If you wanted to be a Coke vendor, dispensing it from your soda fountain, you would be wise to consult your vending guide.

Woodruff was the first to recognize that the fleet of trucks delivering the company's product was, essentially, a moving billboard, and decreed that all should look alike. The letterhead, the envelopes, the uniforms of factory workers—all were strictly dictated from Coca-Cola headquarters.

By the late 1920s, Woodruff had established an actual standardization committee whose job it was to oversee the adherence to the company's standards and messaging.

"It was their charge," says Phil Mooney, retired archivist for the company, "to establish uniformity within the system, so that consumers could focus on the brand."

Woodruff was the new guy in the company, but he had a clear idea of how the business would flourish: "If we are to grow, we have to do certain things. We have to create, within the consumer's mind, a vision of what Coca-Cola looks like."

As Ray Kroc did for McDonald's, Woodruff perfected the algorithm that would enable Coca-Cola to become the company's first billion-dollar brand.

Beyond Scale

For more than a hundred years, the patterns that the founders established and standardized worked magnificently to scale the company. By 2000, the company was in two hundred countries, putting Coca-Cola and three other billion-dollar brands—Diet Coke, Fanta, and Sprite—"within arm's reach of desire." By that time, the company had also begun to expand its portfolio of products to include juice, coffee, and sports drinks.

In 2001, the company's management decided that it would become a total beverage company. This changed everything.

Simultaneously, the environment in which Coca-Cola was doing business was also changing, becoming more challenging and complex.

The collision of a new business model and a more volatile environment had profound implications on the way Coca-Cola used design to grow.

Now, it needed an approach that would allow it to be nimble, to adapt to internal and external conditions that were constantly in flux. If the company wanted to build the next set of billion dollar brands—in juice, in coffee, in water—it needed to figure out how to combine its expertise in designing for scale with a new aptitude: designing for agility.

Little did the company realize, at the turn of the millennium, just how complex the world would become, and how the disruptive challenges it—and all other businesses—would face in the coming decade and beyond would force it to confront design problems of a totally different magnitude.

CHAPTER 3

Complexity

We have entered a period of transition from the world we know toward one we can't yet map.

Ian Bremmer, *Every Nation for Itself*

The word *innovation* can be a black hole. Everyone has an opinion about what it is. You can spend hours, days, even years getting lost inside its constantly morphing layers of meaning.

Search Amazon for books on the subject and you'll find over 60,000 titles. There are books on the other side of innovation, the art of innovation, the ten types of innovation, the myths of innovation, and thousands on some new kind of innovation process.

I'm convinced that, in reality, no one really cares about innovation. What CEOs, management teams, and shareholders really care about is what innovation can generate—growth. That's the whole purpose of innovation—to create sustainable growth. The very nature of capitalism is Darwinian: survival of the fittest. To stay alive, companies must continue to grow.

So, when it comes to innovation, I like to keep things simple and think in terms of growth. *If we change this, or make that thing, do this deal, or launch this program, what kind of growth will it create? Incremental or exponential? Is this a 10 percent or 10x kind of opportunity? Does it have the potential to create slow but predictable growth, or big, fast, unpredictable growth?* This approach cuts straight to the point and saves an amazing number of emails, meetings, calls, Power Point presentations, and consulting fees.

There isn't any magic to this: Replacing the word *innovation* with the word *growth* doesn't make the basic challenge any easier. Creating growth for any business in any industry and in any country, is still *really* hard, because the context for growth is changing dramatically.

Context Is Everything

In chapter 2, we focused on scale, specifically as to how design can help create scale. If we've done our job, all this discussion of design, scale, and systems is starting to make sense conceptually, but no one runs a business in a vacuum based on frameworks, theories, or abstract growth strategies.

If you're a public company, there's nothing conceptual about the pressure of forecasting growth and then meeting analysts' and shareholders' expectations every quarter. If you miss too many times, heads roll all the way down the line.

If you're in a startup, there's nothing conceptual about watching all your funding dry up just when you figure out your next pivot. Unless you get more funding, you're done: The idea that was going to change the world, and all the blood, sweat, and tears that went into it, are gone, just like that.

That's the problem. Your business has a context: Your industry, your customers, your competitors, the economy, and the government all combine to create the context in which your company operates. It's that context that creates the daily grind of creating growth especially difficult.

Now, before we tackle designing for growth in a volatile context, let's acknowledge the obvious: It's always been difficult to launch and sustain a successful company. It's no revelation that the world is complicated. Markets are created. Markets are destroyed. Supply and demand rules. Winners take all. However, there are a few things that are fundamentally different today from doing business ten, twenty, or thirty years ago.

Our world is more complex than ever.

This complexity is making it harder for every business to grow. When most companies talk about getting serious, they generally focus on efficiency. They buckle down; they rebase what's worked in the past. But, in today's world, what used to be called getting back to basics doesn't always work. What used to take discipline now takes a new, different skill set. Marketers used to have to be deft in building brands. Now, they must be experts in *social listening*. Listening and reacting quickly is everything. CEOs used to write their annual letter to the shareholders. Now, they're expected to tweet, blog, and speak directly to an exponentially expanding group of stakeholders. Your management team used to worry about taking costs out of your supply chain and meeting monthly sales targets. They still have to do that, but they also worry about big societal problems like climate change, cyber security, political upheaval, and women's empowerment.

This new complexity is flattening the competitive advantages enjoyed by many companies for decades. As Warren Buffett likes to note, the "moats" that provided protection around century-old companies are drying up quickly. Every multinational looks at one-time industry leaders like Nokia, Sony, and Research in Motion, for fear of having its industry disrupted and its own competitive advantages wiped out.

There's another shift that's made things difficult. It's now easier than ever to be an entrepreneur. Almost anyone, in any part of the world, can start a new business. The barriers to entry for most industries are lower than ever before. This has created a huge global startup community. That sounds great, until you realize that every startup has to worry about the *next* startup. Just look at Facebook. Despite being the world's largest social network, it couldn't rest on its laurels. Rather than try to build competing services, it snapped up Instagram, then WhatsApp, for staggering prices. Every startup is just trying to make it to the other side of profitability while looking in its rear-view mirror.

No one can afford to coast. Every brand, every company, and every industry is ripe for disruption, even total destruction. But the way a company designs can help it adapt.

Before we delve into how that process works, let's explore what we mean by *complexity,* and why it's a good thing for your business. To do that, let's take a quick look at three macrorealities that are making innovation and growth harder for everyone.

Complicated or Complex?

We'd all agree that running even a small business is complicated. You have to worry about competition, profitability, customer relationships, attracting and retaining great people, government regulations, taxes, sourcing, and supply chains.

If you want to grow your business, you'll face even more complications. Instead of having one office or factory, you'll now have several; instead of competing in one market, you'll compete in many. However, it's the issues beyond the company's control—data hacking, social media's influence on your brand, economic conditions in faraway places, the disruptions wrought by extreme weather—that make growing a business not just complicated, but complex.

Are these more word games? You say *tomato*, and I say *tomahto*? Let's make sure we're clear on the meaning of the two words before we go any further.

When something is complicated, it's difficult to understand. When something is complex, it has many different connected parts.

When something is complicated, it's often frustrating to try to make sense of it. Keeping up with local tax laws; sorting through state, local, and national regulations for your industry; figuring out how to manage healthcare for your employees; planning the right balance of traditional and social media in your marketing plan; can all be complicated.

When a topic is complex, it's something that has many different and connected parts. We often use the terms interchangeably but they are quite different. Something can be complex, but still easy to understand. While complicated is almost invariably bad, complexity can be a good thing.

Consider this: Today's smart phone reportedly has more processing power than the computers in the first rocket that carried a man to the moon. I haven't yet found the app to launch a trip to Mars but, like you, I use my phone to call, Skype, text, email, search, listen to music, watch a movie, play a game, take a photo, check the weather, read a book, order car service, find a restaurant, and manage my bank accounts. That requires an incredible amount of complexity. Compare that with my first mobile phone, circa 1995. I bought a Motorola StarTAC flip phone with a three-year plan. It was a model of simplicity since it could only do one thing: Make calls. Now, I not only love my phone's complexity, I've come to depend on it.

Being complicated—confusing, difficult to understand—is never a good thing, but complexity is just the reality of today's world. This difference may seem small, but it's important to understand when it comes to design.

Sometimes, More Is More

Design can make complicated things simpler. You don't have to be a professional designer to get this; it's easy to recognize the difference between good and bad design.

Most of the time, using the approach to design that we discussed in chapter 2—simplifying, standardizing, and integrating—makes complicated things easier to understand, easier to make, and easier to do.

Less choice creates more control and more consistency.
It's design's oldest adage: Less is more, right? Not always.
What about those times when more means more?

What happens when you actually *want* a lot of choices?

I remember the first time I went online in 1995. At the time, there were only about 100,000 Web sites. Today, there are over 700 million and, in many ways, our lives are better because of that vast, easily accessible trove of information. Sometimes, more *is* more.

This was exactly the issue Coca-Cola faced when it shifted its growth strategy. Let's take a look at how complexity connects to growth from the inside out.

In 2001, when the company's CEO first articulated the new growth strategy to move from a company focused on sparkling beverages to a total beverage company, the decision made a lot of strategic sense.

The beverage industry was exploding; the company's context was expanding. Consumers wanted a *lot* more choices. If you're a beverage company, that's a *very* good thing, and a huge opportunity for growth.

At first, the idea of transitioning into a total beverage company doesn't sound like such a leap. You get it: Coca-Cola used to sell Coke and Diet Coke. Now it wants to sell other beverages. No problem.

But this is different. This is like Nike saying it's going to be a total shoe company, offering everything from its iconic Air Force 1 to stilettos, tap shoes, slippers, and boots. That means taking on a whole new competitive set—from Jimmy Choo to Ugg. This is as if Nike said it intended to be *the* shoe company, offering *any* type of shoe to *anyone* in the world.

Given the Coca-Cola Company's mission "to refresh the world," this shift in strategy seems quite sensible—even logical. It created the soft-drink category, and built one of the world's most valuable brands. It seemed reasonable to expect that it could do the same in new, adjacent categories.

But this shift in strategy created massive complexity.

Attempting to lead in all those different categories represented a seismic shift for the company. As we'll see, a total beverage company must design differently from a single beverage company. In fact, the design approach the company used to create and scale Coca-Cola into the brand that it is today, actually complicated its growth in these other categories. The way the company thought about innovation needed to expand to enable its new growth strategy.

Over the last one hundred years, the company has designed very scalable systems for its sparkling brands. They were perfectly designed to scale. Each piece of the business connects perfectly with the next—

from the sourcing of the ingredients, and the manufacturing and distribution of the products, all the way down to sales and marketing. There are, of course, some nuances in different countries due to regulations and cultural tastes, but the company uses the same basic patterns everywhere in the world to get the same level of quality, profit margin, and market share. This is how it ensures that a Coke is a Coke in Taipei or Tunisia or Tallahassee. People often wonder how the company can pull this off on such a massive scale, but there's no magic in it: the business was simply designed to do this.

But other categories, like juice, coffee, or tea, are very different. Rather than being formula based, they are recipe based. There's a big difference between the two.

Take orange juice, for example. Not many people realize that The Coca-Cola Company is actually the world's biggest juice company. About one out of every six oranges grown globally is used by the company to make orange juice.

Designing a billion-dollar juice brand begins with the supply chain. Acquiring the ingredients for those brands would seem to be a no-brainer: Just buy a *lot* of oranges, bottle the juice, then send it out to the world, just the way it is done with Coca-Cola. If only it were that easy!

Orange juice is surprisingly complex.

To start, no one actually knows exactly what kind of orange supply will be available each year. The company works with the world's largest orange farmers, but even *they* don't know how many or even what kind of oranges their groves will produce each season—it's always a best guess. Like wine or coffee, the taste of each individual orange can vary depending on soil conditions, rain, or ripeness when harvested.

This means the company needs to blend different types of oranges to get the taste and quality it's looking for. In short, Coca-Cola blends its supply to a recipe with each batch, just as a vintner does to produce a consistent taste for his cabernet or chardonnay.

On top of this, when it comes to taste, different people prefer different kinds of orange juice. Some people like their OJ with 100 percent juice (less water, more oranges). Some people like the taste of orange but want a more refreshing version (more water, fewer oranges). Some people want bubbles in their juice, some people don't. Some people like bits of orange in their juice, others don't. Then, there are regional preferences in taste: some countries like their orange juice quite sweet; others prefer it tarter. You get the idea. Each of these variations requires a completely different supply chain, manufacturing process, pricing model, merchandising capability, marketing strategy, and distribution system, for *each country*. All of that multiplied by more than two hundred countries gives you more than new billion dollar brands—it gives you complexity.

The problems don't stop there. There's the ongoing headache of the weather, which is getting more extreme every year. There's the problem of colony collapse in the bee population that pollinates the groves. There's the scourge of *citrus greening*, a bacterial disease spread by tiny insects that has devastated crops throughout Florida.

Then, consider that the peak orange growing season is only about three months long, but demand is twelve months a year. Multiply all those problems across the globe, and you begin to understand why the company needs a different approach to design billion-dollar brands in different categories.

Now, remember the goal: Coca-Cola aspires to be the leader in every category (including all the subcategories) in more than two hundred countries.

To stay competitive, it needed an incredible amount of flexibility and adaptability from grove to shelf, from its supply chain to the way it merchandises its products at the point of sale. Its still (nonsparkling) categories are actually very dynamic and require much more agility across the whole value chain.

The problem was the way Coca-Cola designed: It was accustomed to using design to simplify and standardize— not expand. Its approach to design actually made things more complicated: The way it designed as a company was creating confusion and inhibiting growth.

The company needed a new approach, different from the integrated systems approach we discussed in chapter 2. The approach it had used to grow Coca-Cola for almost one hundred years was based on simplifying and standardizing every element—every *thing* and *behavior*—then integrating them seamlessly to make it easier to scale.

With orange juice, and other recipe-based beverages, it couldn't do that. Try as you might, you simply can't standardize an orange. It needed a much more flexible approach. Its design strategy for those brands and products needed to allow it to adapt very quickly as conditions change, as they invariably do.

Of course, it still needed to keep doing what it had always done with Coca-Cola and its other sparkling brands. But it also needed an approach that was more specific to still beverages. The company's growth depended on it.

In part 2, we'll go into this approach in depth. However, there is one more thing we need to discuss. At this point, you still may be tempted to think that this whole agility thing is something only big companies need to worry about. Deciding to be *the total X company* is not your growth strategy and probably never will be. But what is common to every business—from startups to multinationals—is the tectonic shift happening in the external context of every industry. *No market, no country, no* industry is immune. Every company's growth today is pegged to how successfully it can remain relevant and adapt to a rapidly changing environment.

Everyone Needs Agility

Let's take a quick look at three new realities that create more complexity for everyone—from the startup that launched yesterday to the century-old multinational. These new realities affect the type of problems that all companies face today, making it harder than ever to grow.

Reality #1: We are surrounded by wicked problems.

Earlier we talked about how complexity affects companies at a high level. But when problems become wicked problems, then complexity goes into overdrive.

The term *wicked problems* originated in the world of social planning to describe problems that can't be solved by mathematical formulas or trial and error. They're often ill-defined, are dependent on a number of often uncontrollable variables, and have no so-called right or optimal solutions.

Wicked problems are highly complex—they have many connected issues with no single solution.

Examples might include such things as political upheaval (a new, unpredictable leader in North Korea), economic turmoil (the Euro zone debt crisis or the slowdown in growth in China), and natural disasters (from earthquakes in Turkey to shifts in weather patterns that cause drought in some areas of a region and floods in others).

Everyone is affected by wicked problems: people, governments, and companies. However, if you're a company, some wicked problems not only disrupt your business, but can fundamentally change your industry, significantly challenging your long-term goals and short-term results.

After a building serving as space for several factories collapsed in Bangladesh in 2013, for example, American and European clothing manufacturers had to rethink their responsibility for factory conditions in the countries in which their garments were manufactured. In 2009, in response to the wicked problem of e-waste (the disposal of massive quantities of outdated consumer electronics like computers, cellphones, and television sets) in developing countries, several large computer manufacturers banned the export of nonworking electronics to those nations. Recently, in response to the growing problem of highway accidents involving mobile phones, four big cell-phone companies joined forces in a million-dollar ad campaign to stop texting while driving.

Big companies are affected by wicked problems but can't solve them; all they can do is use their reach, relationships, and considerable resources to do their best to help chip away at them.

Not all wicked problems are social or related to the environment. The so-called war for talent is a great example. Most startup founders know that high failure rates are often the result of not having the right team. But how do you know exactly *when* to staff up? And when you do decide it's time, how can you get the best talent when every other startup is fighting for the same people? Do you have the *right* incentives? And just *how* flexible is your staffing model?

If you're inside a big company, you must continue to evolve your culture, so that you can retain your current staff but also recruit the next generation. By 2020, half of all workers will be millennials—the most educated and culturally diverse of any generation, who are also notorious job-hoppers who dislike bureaucracy and distrust traditional hierarchies.

Both startups and big companies worry about whether they're evolving their hiring strategies fast enough. How much is enough? Are you building the kind of culture you need for today and tomorrow? Where should you source talent? Should you try new, supposed open models? And what about the education system—who's responsible for ensuring we're training the next generation for the kind of business challenges we see coming?

Ignoring wicked problems is not an option.

Wicked problems are always complex and always confusing. Dealing with them can generate a lot of costs, take up a lot of time, and, if you're not careful, can cause your growth strategy to go sideways. But as much as you might be tempted, they cannot be ignored. They're not going away, and they're beyond our ability to fix permanently.

Like all other multinationals, The Coca-Cola Company is affected by many wicked problems, in different ways, around the world. And, like others, it recognizes that it can't grow its business unless it becomes part of the solution. One problem that's gotten a lot of attention is the wicked problem of obesity, especially in developed countries.

While the growth rate in the percentage of the population considered obese now seems to be stabilizing, it's still unacceptably high. What makes this problem wicked is that it's a result of many connected problems. Research suggests many interrelated issues including more sedentary lifestyles, excessive portion sizes, and even, some scientists speculate, the presence of certain bacteria in our digestive systems.

Governments and NGOs also understand that they too must be

part of the solution, but ultimately they can't solve the problem alone either. The Coca-Cola Company is tackling the issue on many different levels, with partnerships around the world.

Still, as the company's CEO, Muhtar Kent, has said, "Obesity is a global societal problem which will take all of us working together. We are committed to being part of the solution, working closely with partners from business, government and civil society."

One of the most global wicked problems that affects Coca-Cola's business and the communities in which it operates is water.

Water is the main ingredient in all of Coca-Cola's beverages, so for the company, it's more than a nice-to-have. It's Coca-Cola's most precious resource.

So, too, with the general population. Healthy watersheds and access to safe water and sanitation enable health, education, security, and economic development for people around the world, but the pressures converging on the world's freshwater supplies are significant. Dramatic population growth, economic development, urbanization, and climate change all combine to stress our shared water resources.

That makes water a wicked problem on many dimensions. There's the issue of scarcity, of quality, of pricing, of policy, of flooding, of climate change, and of infrastructure, to name but a few. These problems are interconnected, and defy easy solutions, not just by companies, but by countries and continents as well.

From population growth to climate change, the pressures on water are increasing exponentially.

When it comes to water, it's easy to see that the company can't grow its business unless it becomes part of the solution. So, in 2010, it outlined an ambitious goal when it comes to water stewardship. Its goal is to be *water-neutral* by 2020—to safely return to nature and to communities an amount of water equivalent to that which it uses in all its beverages and their production by 2020. All of Coca-Cola's projects, since the goal was announced, are designed to connect to help it reach this goal.

As Coca-Cola's CEO told *Forbes Magazine*, there wasn't one "eureka!" moment when the company recognized that sustainability was important to its business strategy. When it first started out, Coca-Cola had the usual warm-and-fuzzy words about sustainability in its corporate responsibility report. There were no metrics to see whether any of this was working. It wasn't connected to all the parts of the business.

"We also didn't have proper alignment with our bottling partners," Kent said. "The first prerequisite of being successful [at The Coca-Cola Company] is that you work as a global system. Second, it's got to be embedded in the business plan. Third, you've got to have the right metrics around it; it's got to be measurable. And then it's got to be beneficial from a financial perspective.

"We have learned one basic lesson," he said, "and that is that unless it is synonymous—business and planet—it doesn't get traction."

To begin resolving those disconnects, the company began linking its growth strategy to its water stewardship goal. As the company's business grows, so does its investment in community water partnerships that help it achieve its 2020 goal and beyond.

To date, Coca-Cola has close to five hundred water projects in development around the world. All of these are designed to connect to create as much impact as possible on the wicked problem of water.

Addressing such challenges often ups the cost of doing business exponentially. Yet, for companies to be successful and grow in today's world, they must play a role in helping to solve the wicked problems to which they are connected.

One of the tools that Coca-Cola uses to visualize wicked problems is called a *mind map*. The company didn't invent this tool, in fact, it's quite common; there are lots of examples online. The specific tool is not important; what's important is finding a way to visualize all of the related issues so that everyone can *see* and understand the complexity.

LESSON LEARNED #5

Make a Mind Map

One of the hardest things for managers at any company to do is to see all the issues related to a problem. The more complex the problem, the more difficult it is. In chapter 1 we said, "Design is about intentionally connecting things to solve problems."

> *What do you do if you don't know all the things that need to be connected?*

You make a mind map. A mind map is a term for a diagram that is intended to help you and everyone on your team see all the related elements and behaviors for any given problem or opportunity. The best mind maps are actually designed together as a group, with each team member building on one another's thoughts to ultimately visualize the interrelated problems.

> *Mind maps not only help you see all the related issues but they also help to get everyone on the same page, with a common language and collective buy-in.*

There's no standard way to make a mind map. You can doodle one on a Post-it note, create one in Power Point, or scribble ideas on a big white board. There are also quite a few apps you can buy that are designed specifically to make mind maps. The value is in the result, not in how you get there.

Step 1: Get everyone in the same room.

Get your core group of stakeholders together (you and whoever else will be working on the project). I like to use a big piece of paper, from a flip-chart pad. I also like to use Post-it notes and Sharpie pens, so I get enough for everyone.

Step 2: Get all the issues on the table.

Brainstorm all of the various issues, concepts, themes, elements, behaviors, regulations, etc. related to the problem you're trying to solve. Ask everyone to write each one of them on a Post-it note. Try to capture the issue in two to three words—as few as possible.

For example, if we're trying to wrap our heads around a wicked problem as complex as water scarcity, many different issues surface, ranging from global to local, economic to social and ethical, to environmental issues.

To keep things moving, I give everyone ten to fifteen minutes or so to capture all the various issues that they feel are important. Next, I ask everyone to put all their Post-its on one of the clean sheets of big paper.

Step 3: Quickly group the related issues.

Then, I ask a couple of people to begin grouping all of the related issues together by moving all of the Post-it notes around until they are in several smaller groups. Don't worry if they are not ideally grouped. Just do it as quickly as you can to try to get to your metalevel groups of related topics. Then, we discuss as a group to see if everyone thinks that we've captured most of the issues. I've found it's best to take a short break at this point.

Step 4: Connect everything.

While people are out of the room, I like to use a clean piece of paper, draw a big circle in the middle with the problem we're focused on (water scarcity, for example), and then draw three or four more circles around your main issue representing the three or four metalevel issues.

Next, move all the Post-its that relate to that topic around it, and draw lines or arrows connecting those issues to the larger one. Most of the issues are actually subsets of others. Again, it's not important to be 100 percent perfect and debate the exact relationships; what's important is just to be able to see how all the issues that the team brainstormed connect to something, and are not isolated issues. The only critical thing is to keep the most important issues nearer the center and the less important ones closer to the edge of your map.

Step 5: Step back and look for patterns.

After you've connected everything, ask the team to look at the map to determine if you've missed anything. If so, add it. Once you feel as though you're finished, use the map to discuss the patterns that you see, the biggest risks, or the aha revelations that always come out of an exercise like this. Your mind map can help you, as a team, prioritize what needs to be solved first, get a better grip on how long this will take, and identify who else needs to be a part of designing the solution.

Key Takeaway: When you're trying to solve a big, complex problem, mind maps can help you visualize and prioritize the issues you must take into account in designing a solution.

Reality #2: We live in an After-Internet world.

"Everything is changing: you, your family, your education, your neighborhood, your job, your government, your relation to others. And they're changing dramatically. All media work us over completely. They are so pervasive in their personal, political, economic, aesthetic, psychological, moral, ethical and social consequences that they leave no part of us untouched, unaffected, unaltered. The medium is the message."

Marshall McLuhan, the futurist, wrote that in 1967, before the invention of the Internet. The interconnected, media-saturated environment we now live in is one that not even McLuhan could have imagined.

Today's world is open sourced, collaborative, dynamic, two way, cocreated, always on, constantly evolving, shifting, linked, fluid, and changing every second of the day.

I remember the first time I went online. It was 1995. At the time, I was reading *Being Digital*, by Nicolas Negroponte, founder of MIT's famed Media Lab. It reframed the way I thought about the world. Essentially, the book suggests that anything and everything will eventually shift from being made of atoms to bits: One day, everything that can be, will be digitized, then connected. With eBooks, ecommerce, online banking, digitized photography and music, streaming video, and an always-on news cycle, it's evident that we're well on our way. This shift is changing everything.

Some fifteen years later, one of Negroponte's Media Lab successors, entrepreneur, investor, college dropout, and Internet visionary Joi Ito updated Negroponte's predictions with his own forecasts as to where we're heading in what he calls the *After-Internet* (AI) world.

According to Ito, one of the biggest disruptors for established businesses is that the cost of innovation, collaboration, and distribution
has decreased significantly. That means that big companies no longer
have a monopoly because of their capital resources, factories, or net-
works. A couple of guys with a big idea in Bangalore can go to Startup
Weekend for one hundred dollars, rent a desk in a coworking space
for five hundred dollars per month (27,345 rupees), buy some space
in Amazon's cloud, and possibly disrupt companies that have huge assets and have been around for decades. This is what an After-Internet
world looks like.

In 2013, for example, a seventeen-year-old Australian teenager
living in England built a content-shortening app, called *Summly*, in
his bedroom, which he promptly sold to Yahoo for a reported thirty
million dollars. Now, imagine the next seventeen-year-old with a 3D
printer, and you begin to sense the dimensions of the potential upheaval.

What's more, these same young entrepreneurs don't need the per-
mission of an organization to act on their ideas.

---

*For companies to compete they need to adopt the
same mindset—living in an after-Internet world
reduces competitive advantages many companies
have enjoyed in the before-Internet world.*

Ito offers nine principles that established businesses need to keep in
mind to avoid being rendered obsolete by more nimble competitors.

1. Resilience instead of strength, which means you yield and
   allow failure, and bounce back instead of trying to resist
   failure.

2. Pull instead of push. That means you pull the resources from the network as you need them, as opposed to centrally stocking them and controlling them.
3. Take risk instead of focusing on safety.
4. Focus on the system instead of objects.
5. Have good compasses, not maps.
6. Work on practice instead of theory, because sometimes you don't know why it works, but what is important is that it is working, not that you have some theory around it.
7. Practice disobedience instead of compliance. You don't get a Nobel Prize for doing what you are told. Too much of school is about obedience, we should really be celebrating disobedience.
8. It's the crowd, not the experts.
9. Focus on learning instead of education.

While all of these principles have the potential to be disruptive—or instructive—for big companies, the last two principles that Ito articulated are particularly relevant as companies try to connect with their customers.

The mandate to pay attention to the crowd, not the experts, and to focus on learning, not education, has never been more essential.

The crowd, after all, now has the power to build you up, or tear you down. We've all seen what happens when a disgruntled and motivated tweeter marshals her 140 characters in a campaign against a company's products. Or when a galvanized audience takes to Facebook to either promote—or condemn—a product, a company, or an initiative they may or may not like.

Facebook itself saw how an activated citizenry could foil its plans for a strategic move that would have been great for its advertising revenue, but not so great for its users' privacy. In 2012, for example, the company had to repeatedly dial back some of its changes, after users and the federal government objected to invasions of privacy. Airbnb has gotten in trouble with various municipalities over laws prohibiting short-term rentals of apartments or houses.

When we talk about an after-Internet world, we must factor in the social web. Gone are the days when a company could assume that its customers would docilely follow its lead. Now, those same customers want a voice, and are eager to call out brands they like—or revile.

Designing for this new world is an ongoing challenge, given its extreme fluidity and volatility. But, as any Borg will tell you, resistance is futile. Adapt, or suffer the consequences.

Reality #3: Winning is about creating shared value.

All companies want to grow. There's nothing new about that. What is new is the expanding role that companies have in affecting the growth of the communities in which they operate.

Much has been written about the role of companies in the area of sustainability, especially around environmental concerns. However, more and more, in order to create new value, companies must think much more holistically about value creation beyond simply doing the responsible thing in the geographies in which they do business. Growth must be based on a shared understanding of the goals of everyone involved.

We're all connected.

Governments (local and national) need successful companies to create a strong economy. Big companies need small companies to supply them with goods and services. Small companies need skilled and educated people to work for them. People need government to help provide the education and financial resources to get the skills they need to get jobs. Financial well-being leads to physical well-being. Healthy economies mean healthy communities.

As Coca-Cola's CEO Muhtar Kent says, "Truth is, we can scarcely talk about innovation without growth—as strongly connected as these two ideas are. And that's as it should be. After all, growth makes the world go 'round. Everyone needs to grow. Individuals. Families. Communities. Cities. States. Nations. Continents. All of them. And we need all types of growth. Economic growth. Social growth. Intellectual growth. Political growth. Spiritual growth. And on and on. Because growth is, ultimately, the way I believe we will overcome the great challenges of our time."

Truly sustainable companies create not only economic value but also value for the communities in which they operate. Michael Porter and Mark Kramer call this *shared value*.

"Companies must take the lead in bringing business and society back together," they say. "Businesses must reconnect company success with social progress. Shared value is not social responsibility, philanthropy, or even sustainability, but a new way to achieve economic success. It is not on the margin of what companies do, but at the center."

You have to create value in all areas of a company's activities to win—for you and for your suppliers, your customers, your consumers, your community.

Recently, Coca-Cola launched just such an initiative, promoting recycling, in partnership with the American musician and producer will.i.am. In 2008, the former Black Eyed Peas frontman was attending a meeting of the Clinton Global Initiative, the former president's social change foundation, when he heard about the movement to create a world with zero waste. The idea connected. For years, the rapper had been distressed by the amount of trash left behind in the stadiums, arenas, and clubs where he and his group played. "I had brought people together," he said, "but they left behind so much waste."

The sight of all that debris—especially PET packaging—bothered him, but the Clinton event spurred a thought: What if all those plastic bottles could be turned into clothes and bags and shoes that people loved? What if you could turn aluminum cans into bicycles? More important, what if, by wearing or buying such products, you could show you care by what you wear? Would that be enough to get people to take recycling more seriously?

Later that year, he began creating a handcrafted book describing what such a recycling program might look like and, in 2009, he reached out to us to see if we were interested in forging a partnership.

There was an immediate bond. "It captured the hearts and minds of Coke executives," says Bea Perez, the company's vice president and chief sustainability officer. More important, the idea aligned with the company's own goals around zero waste by 2020, and gave it a way to get that message out in a fresh and relevant way.

"Only about thirty percent of Americans recycle," says Perez, a number that reflects both a lack of awareness of the issue and a dearth of convenient places to put recyclable waste products. It was a wicked problem that the company needed help in solving.

A partnership with will.i.am would help with something that was critical in generating interest in recycling: Shift the idea from being the responsible thing to do, to being the *cool* thing to do.

In 2012, during the London Olympics, will.i.am and Coca-Cola launched the lifestyle brand EKOCYCLE with a commercial that combined will.i.am's hit song, "Love," with the message, "the end can be a new start."

EKOCYCLE's Facebook page pointed readers to places where they could find recycling facilities, and launched the brand's first products—Beats headphones by Dr. Dre, which incorporate recycled PET into their manufacturing process, and New Era caps. Later that year, four more companies: Case-Mate, a line of cases for smartphones; Levi's jeans; MCM, a manufacturer of high-end handbags, luggage, and leather goods; and RVCA, a surf/skate fashion brand, signed on.

Designing to Connect

In chapter 1, we said that *design is about intentionally connecting things to solve problems.* If you want to use design to help your company grow, then the question you need to ask is: "Is the way we're designing as a company—our approach to design—flexible enough to handle things like wicked problems? Is the way we're designing maximizing the crowd? Are we designing in a way that enables shared value? If not, why not? And, what if we could?"

These are not easy questions for most companies; they don't fit into the normal operations of the business. There are thorny issues like: Who owns the responsibility of creating shared value in the organization? Which team? Which function? They all do, right? But where is creating shared value in each person's job description? And who can anticipate initiatives like ECOCYCLE in the normal business planning cycle when budgets are allocated for the next year or two?

Design can help. By starting with the *Why*—to design on purpose and be very intentional about the way you do it as a company—you can begin to connect the dots, build synergy, and connect silos.

Design isn't owned by one department, function, or guru.

Nobody *owns* design. Designing is all about connecting and it takes a lot of connecting to create growth in today's world.

And that's the point: To undertake these kinds of initiatives, the way a company designs must enable agility, not just scale. All companies need scale but without agility, they can't create what every business needs even more—*relevance*.

LESSON LEARNED #6

Think Big, Start Small

Imagine that it's day one on your new job, where your mandate is to create a design-driven culture for your company. What do you do first? Unless you're the new CEO, you may have a few big ideas, but without earning a certain level of trust and establishing a track record, it's really hard to do anything very ambitious. So where do you start? Small.

Look for someone (a person, a team, etc.) with a problem and work with them to solve it. In the beginning, this is the only way to get traction. It doesn't really matter much what the project is; you just need a proof point and some momentum.

I remember one of the first teams that reached out to me at Coca-Cola was one of our teams in China, who were trying to launch a brand called *Qoo*. Originally designed in Japan, Qoo is a noncarbonated juice that comes in fruity flavors, and has a cheery, pale-blue mascot who says, "Qoo!" when it takes a sip. ("Qoo" means "Ahh" in

Japanese—what most people say when they drink some-thing that immediately quenches their thirst.)

I hopped a plane to Hong Kong, and joined a workshop to discuss what we could do.

Normally, the group assembled to address a problem like this would include marketers, technical people (flavor scientists, etc), packaging engineers, commercial teams (who figure out the manufacturing and distribution logis-tics), and customer teams (who determine which of our retailers were the likeliest outlets). This was the first time that design was invited to the table.

It wasn't too long before I figured out that they ex-pected me to talk about branding—a natural assumption. However, I could begin to see the real opportunity for de-sign was to help in connecting all these disparate pieces. We'd have to change the mindset of design from being a way of making stuff look prettier to being a way of con-necting all of the teams and activities contributing to the launch. That was the real opportunity.

While the problem of launching a new brand in a dif-ferent country is always difficult, at the time, I remember feeling as though our work on Qoo was *very* small compared to what we could be doing on Coca-Cola. But, through this experience, I began to form relationships with our teams working in China and get some traction.

By the time the Beijing Olympic Games came around, four years later, we were really able to leverage design in a powerful way. This included sponsoring a national compe-tition with design students to create limited edition alumi-num bottles interpreting eight themes from our Coke Side of Life campaign.

This had never been done in China. The program was so successful that the packaging began selling on eBay for over one hundred dollars per bottle. We launched the celebration with a giant party with hundreds of people, including our chairman, the students, and DJs from around the world in the middle of Beijing.

I remember sitting there thinking to myself that four years ago I could have never imagined this happening. And I could draw a straight line back to working on that little brand called Qoo. Ahhhhh.

Key Takeaway: In the beginning, create quick wins and build relationships.

PART 2

Designing for Agility

There are millions of brands in the world, and many are successful. But only a few make it to billion-dollar status—a special club of brands that have a market value of at least one billion dollars. While it's getting easier than ever to create a brand of this magnitude, it's getting harder than ever to keep one.

For shareholders, billion-dollar brands are not only highly lucrative, but a very tangible sign of a company's innovation capability and culture.

Why? Billion-dollar brands only stay that way by finding new ways to create competitive advantage and relevance. Resting on your laurels in today's world is an open invitation for disruption.

Most billion-dollar brands lead their categories and a lucky few become symbolic of the highest level of quality and trust. Some even transcend their product association to become what Harvard marketing professor Douglas Holt calls *cultural icons,* which are infused with cultural myth and meaning.

The famous commercial from the 1970s, in which Pittsburgh Steelers' defensive tackle Mean Joe Greene tossed his jersey to the kid who offered him a Coke, was about a lot more than just the satisfaction of a cold beverage after a tough game. It captured the social tension of the times, and Coca-Cola, a brand, actually communicated its point of view.

This kind of cultural cachet is the Holy Grail for most brands—but even that kind of prestige no longer guarantees long-term survival.

As consumers, we don't really think of billion-dollar brands in terms of their market value. We just think of them as the best brands in the world.

Even so, the size of some of the brands may surprise you. For instance, Pampers is a $31 billion brand, helping over 25 million babies stay dry every day. It's one of the twenty-three billion-dollar brands owned by P&G, including Duracell, Braun, Bounty, and Gillette.

Oreo is one of Kraft's billion-dollar brands. It's the world's best-selling cookie brand, generating some $1.5 billion in global annual revenues.

Kleenex, one of Kimberly-Clark's billion-dollar brands, is estimated to be worth $3 billion. Every time we say something like, "I need a Kleenex," rather than saying, "I need a high-quality tissue product," we affirm its category and cultural leadership.

And this, of course, is every company's dream.

Every brand wants to be in the Billion-Dollar–Brand Club.

The elite Billion-Dollar–Brand Club is largely made up of well-established, time-tested brands, often considered the old guard:

Energizer, Nintendo, Disney, Lego, Visa, L'Oreal, Louis Vuitton, and, of course, Coca-Cola.

As you'd imagine, once a brand gets in the club, it never wants to be shown the door. But it's getting harder every day to maintain membership.

In Part 1 we discussed how the world is changing faster than ever before, and how that is putting a whole new level of pressure on established companies and their billion-dollar brands. As we'll see in Part 2, unless companies, especially big, established companies, can actually *embrace* this complexity by being more agile, they put their billion-dollar brands at risk. One need only to look at what happened to one of the most legendary American companies to see how easy it is not only to lose a billion-dollar brand, but to nearly lose an entire company as well.

Kodak Moment

The Eastman Kodak Company was founded in 1892. Its Brownie camera made capturing a memory easier for everyone. Its portfolio of cameras, projectors, and film drove profits into the company for decades. Kodak was seen as the most innovative company in the world at that time—a nineteenth century mash-up of Apple, Google, and Amazon.

One of the company's brands, Kodak film, became a billion-dollar brand, the name most people associated with the highest quality of film, and how most Americans preserved and cherished memories. For most people, Kodak and film were synonymous—they wouldn't think of using another brand.

The phrase "Kodak moment" was embedded deep into the American vernacular, representing the perfect instant to capture a memory (on Kodak film). Some of America's most unforgettable moments were captured on Kodak film: A sailor in Times Square celebrating the end of World War II by sweeping a stranger into a passionate kiss, NASA astronauts stepping onto the surface of the moon, the assassination of JFK. As the company scaled its global operations, so did the idea of a Kodak moment. The idea jumped the country's borders and went global.

Paul Simon immortalized photographers' passion for the product with his song, "Kodachrome," which lauded the film's "nice bright colors," and implored, "Mama, don't take my Kodachrome away!"

But, in January 2012, the Eastman Kodak Company took everybody's Kodachrome away when it filed for bankruptcy. It had dwindled to 19,000 employees, and was delisted from the stock exchange with a stock price under one dollar. A little over a decade before, it had had over 145,000 employees and was one of the fabled thirty Dow Jones blue chip stocks trading at over eight dollars per share.

It has emerged from bankruptcy and is gradually regaining its footing, but it's unlikely ever to be the behemoth it was in its heyday.

What happened? How could such an innovative company fail? As we see other great companies struggle to avoid a similar fate, it's clear that the ability to adapt to a changing marketplace is more important than ever.

Every company is at risk of having a Kodak moment.

Wait a minute. How can such a highly *innovative* company implode so spectacularly? How can one of its brands get to billion-dollar status, then, almost overnight, become irrelevant? Like all the companies in the Billion-Dollar Club, Kodak leveraged the power of design to scale, but it was no longer enough. Kodak is not alone. Some of the world's most successful brands, disrupted by a rapidly changing marketplace, have not only quit growing, but are struggling just to remain viable. For these brands, the name of the game is simply to survive the free fall.

The Upstarts Called Startups

Let's look at this from another angle. There is a whole group of brands out there that *aren't* fighting for survival. They came from very humble beginnings, but almost overnight have made it into the Billion-Dollar–Brand Club. You'd think the old guard would welcome them—not true. In fact, these upstarts are creating chaos and panic in the ranks of their elders. They're not only relevant, but top of mind, for almost everyone.

First of all, these upstarts are *very* young. While most of the old guard members take pride in their century-old reputations, most of the upstarts are fewer than five years old; some are fewer than two. Previously, this lack of wisdom and experience would have kept most of the upstarts off of the potential new members list. Not anymore.

These fledgling brands also look and sound very different from Oreos, Pampers, and Ralph Lauren. They are all about growth that is big and fast, whereas the old guard is mostly about growth that is slow and steady. The old guard, dressed in pinstripes and wing tips to signify their blue-chip status, are predictable and reliable. The upstarts, dressed in t-shirts and jeans, can be brash and irreverent, nimble and unafraid to fail. They make mistakes, pivot, and move on.

Don't confuse startups with the dotcoms.

At the turn of the millennium, the world became fascinated with a bunch of new, fast-growing companies that, at the time, were mostly Internet based. These new-economy companies were quickly dubbed *dotcoms* to differentiate them from established old-economy companies and conventional new, small businesses. By and large, they were highly energized, often risky, neophytes who seemed to have entirely different DNA from either big companies or their more traditional small peers.

They were ambitious and inventive but took their playbooks from the James Dean School of Management—they lived fast and died young. Most burned through millions of dollars of cash building cool Web sites and outfitting offices with Aeron chairs, foosball tables, and celebrity chef kitchens, but often neglected the more prosaic requirements of building a business, like figuring out whether they had a viable product or a scalable business model.

A lot of those high fliers came crashing to earth following the market implosion that began in March 2000. The lessons of that period of dotcom mania were hard won, but indelible for companies that followed. Unlike their predecessors, like Webvan.com, Boo.com, or Pets .com, with their glam launch parties and expensive Super Bowl ads, startups like Airbnb, Square, and Uber started very lean—with little to no cash—and focused on a big unmet need and their business model from day one. By the time they reached billion-dollar status, they had devised and validated a repeatable business model that could challenge the old guard, and even disrupt entire industries. What's important to note is that they were *designed* to do this: to learn, adapt, then scale without going under.

Remember, startups are not smaller versions of big companies. They aren't even small versions of small companies. Startups aren't even companies yet.

A startup is a temporary organization designed to search for a repeatable and scalable business model.

There's a big difference between Brooklyn's Kickstarter and Joe's Barber Shop on West 132nd Street in Harlem. Both have few employees and humble office space, but Kickstarter was actually designed from the cradle to scale from a local brand to at least a national, and perhaps global, brand. Over the course of its first three years, it changed its business model several times to adapt to the market. It updates its product almost weekly. It's growing exponentially. It's challenging old models of investing and quickly spawning new versions of itself creating a whole new industry around crowd-funding.

Not so with Joe's. Joe's was designed to do exactly what great barber shops have always done—provide the best haircuts (and maybe a little gossip) on the block. It's using a business model that's been around forever and it has no plans to change anything, except perhaps upgrading to a new sign or more comfortable chairs. It was simply not designed to disrupt its industry or take on Supercuts, Great Clips, Fantastic Sam's, or some other national chain. Joe's Barber Shop will never launch in Indonesia or Brazil. And I'm sure Joe is just fine with that.

But the way startups use design is different.

The way startups design everything from their products, to their staff, partnerships, and revenue model enables agility.

So, if you're a big, established company with billion-dollar brands, you're likely asking yourself, "Why can't we do this? Why can't big brands do what startups do? Why can't we create the kind of exponential growth startups create?"

The old guard is expert at designing for scale. They've built amazing companies that manage global brands, supply chains, and distribution channels. They have the talent. They have the relationships. They have the money. Yet they struggle to do what startups do. After leading their industries for decades, it just doesn't make sense that a new player could come in and turn an entire market upside down overnight.

Think, for example, of Instagram, the startup that created a mobile photo-sharing network. Facebook bought the fledgling company in 2012 for $1 billion in cash and stock. Instagram went from no revenue and no users to creating a brand valued at $1 billion with over 30 million users in fewer than two years.

Why couldn't Kodak do something like that? It was, after all, the go-to photo brand of choice for a century. The company, despite its decades of market research, priceless intellectual property, a portfolio of billon-dollar brands, and huge R&D capability, evidently didn't have the agility to see the opportunity and act on it swiftly. In 2001, while the founders of Instagram were still in high school, Kodak bought Ofoto, an early version of Instagram, but just couldn't make it work.

The Kodak/Instagram story is the kind of tale that keeps the old guard up at night. Are we leaving any money on the table? Are any of our billion-dollar brands at risk? Is our entire industry ripe for disruption?

The missing capability, as you've doubtless guessed by now, is agility. As we've noted earlier, it never happens by chance—only by design.

Fourth Era of Innovation

Now, imagine if the old guard could somehow figure out how to move with the agility of Square, Dropbox, or Facebook? What would it look like if Sony could leverage its tremendous assets—its reach, resources, and relationships—to create that kind of big, fast growth? Might it take some pressure off the core business and give the company the new revenue streams and relevance it needs to connect with a new generation?

Many people are predicting that we are moving into a new era focused on business-model innovation.

The pressure of this new level of complexity and opportunity is actually creating something unprecedented. In a 2012 article for the *Harvard Business Review*, called "The New Corporate Garage," Scott Anthony, managing director of Clay Christensen's innovation consulting firm, Innosight, called this phenomenon the Fourth Era of Innovation.

It's an era, he writes, in which innovation will be led by big companies. His story goes something like this:

The first era of innovation is known as the Lone Inventor era. That was when individuals like the Wright Brothers, Edison, and chemist John Pemberton were able to bring breakthrough innovations to life. They weren't under a lot of time or competitive pressure—they could work at their own speed using their own resources to get these businesses off the ground.

However, with the perfection of the assembly line, innovation became out of reach for the lone individual. This led to the second era of innovation, the Corporate Labs era. Large enterprises, with big R&D labs, like DuPont, Procter & Gamble, and IBM were responsible for most major commercial inventions.

This led to the third era of innovation, the Venture-Capital–Backed Startups era, which is where we are now. As the story goes, restless employees in big companies, frustrated by corporate hierarchies, inertia, and slow-footedness, band together with other entrepreneurs to start their own companies, often backed by venture capitalists. These aren't just new companies. They're companies with a big purpose and business models that are designed to grow fast—what we now call *startups.*

But this isn't just a Silicon Valley phenomenon or an opportunity only for highly developed markets, like the United States. Today's global startup community reaches from New York to Nepal. There are coworking spaces in every city of the world. There are incubator and accelerator programs in almost every large organization. There are alternative funding vehicles (like crowd-funding) available to all. And there are great organizations, like Startup Weekend, that can train anyone to go from idea to startup in fifty-four hours. All of this has created a giant startup ecosystem, making it easier than ever for anyone to start a business.

It's also easier than ever for competitors to knock off your idea, poach your talent, and cannibalize your market. Groupon, for example, took off like lightning, and reached $1 billion in revenue faster than any other company in history. But rivals in the daily-deal space quickly followed, and Groupon's share price has suffered ever since.

The problem these days comes in sustaining a business long enough to create enduring competitive advantage or scale. And therein lies the seed for the fourth era of innovation. If big companies, with their huge assets and global scale, can adopt new entrepreneurial behaviors—like the agility of a startup—they can actually lead in this new era.

Designing for Agility

So, how can a company use design to create agility? That's what Part 2 is all about.

Designing for agility has a different purpose, a different process, and creates a different kind of product than designing for scale.

We'll take a look at how The Coca-Cola Company uses this approach to be smarter, faster, and leaner, and, in the process, create new value and sustainable growth. We'll demonstrate how your company can do this, too.

CHAPTER 4

Smarter

"Everybody has a plan until they get punched in the mouth."

Mike Tyson, former heavyweight boxing champion

I used to love my BlackBerry. It was simple to use and made email so much easier than using my laptop. I travel a lot, and the sense of mobility it offered was liberating. I would check my mail one last time before takeoff, and check it again as soon as I landed. It seemed fantastic.

Of course, I wasn't alone. A few years ago, BlackBerry devices were so popular that many people referred to them as Crackberries; they were that addictive.

I carried my BlackBerry in the front pocket of my jeans. I remember that when it vibrated, I'd immediately reach for it, like Pavlov's dog. The habit became so intense that some people reported that they could often feel *ghost vibrations*—the sense of a BlackBerry device vibrating even when it wasn't.

From 2004 to 2010, BlackBerry owned the mobile phone market. Fast-forward to today: BlackBerry went from a 50 percent market share to near irrelevance.

What happened? BlackBerry simply couldn't adapt. When the market began to shift from cell phones to smartphones—from a focus on hardware to software innovation, handsets to apps—BlackBerry kept developing hardware solutions.

Why not? It had worked before. They saw what Apple was doing, but chose to stay the course. After all, Apple was a computer company. What did it know about mobile phones? I can imagine a bunch of BlackBerry managers in a conference room dismissing the first iPhone, maybe calling it a toy or vastly inferior, nothing to take seriously. Music, apps, cameras: Why would you bolt them onto a phone? Like most successful companies, BlackBerry focused on flawless execution—on what had worked in the past—designing beautiful handsets and marketing them around the world. They designed for scale, not for agility.

Unlike Apple, BlackBerry didn't understand how to use design to learn and adapt to a rapidly changing marketplace. Frankly, Apple didn't know exactly what would connect with consumers with its first release either. If you bought one of the earliest iPhones, you probably remember that it was very buggy and unreliable. However, this allowed the company to start learning what worked and what didn't very quickly, which made them smarter. What many people don't realize is that this is an essential part of designing for agility.

By designing for agility, companies can learn faster and become smarter, which reduces the risk of being disrupted.

In hindsight, it's easy to see how BlackBerry missed the whole industry shift. Far from being a toy, the iPhone was actually an incredibly smart design decision by Apple. It enabled them to leapfrog into a completely new industry, disrupt it, and take a leadership position—with the speed and destructive power of a startup.

"The world did not stop for BlackBerry, and we're seeing the result of that today," said Bill Kreher, an analyst with Edward Jones. By the time BlackBerry released its Z10 app-based smart phone in 2013, it was far behind the curve—at least two years too late.

It's not like the executives at BlackBerry were oblivious to the world changing outside its doors. I'm sure they had a solid business plan, long-term growth model, and, perhaps, even an inspiring video to boost senior management's confidence. However, unlike much of business history, when a leader could take time to gather data, assess the situation, and map a thoughtful strategic plan, the window that a company has to recognize its mistakes and take corrective action has become stunningly small.

As the stakes get higher, and the world gets more complex, using design to learn and adapt is becoming more and more critical. The environment in which managers must make potentially life-and-death decisions for their companies has never been more difficult.

As the 2012 World Economic Forum recently noted: "The new context in which leaders find themselves is structurally different. It is complex, volatile and uncertain. Most do not feel prepared to manage this complexity. Modern leaders are under constant pressure to make decisions in a high-velocity and information-abundant environment. The pressure to deliver, constant scrutiny, and lack of clarity on the effect of their decisions has resulted in fear of making the wrong choice and decision paralysis."

Disrupt or Be Disrupted

You don't have to be a CEO or head of state to understand this on a personal level. We have all had to make big shifts—pivots—in our careers just to stay relevant. This requires an ability to be quick-witted, combined with the intelligence to see what change is coming, and how your own skills can adapt to an environment that is in constant flux.

In 1995, the big wave on the horizon was the Internet.

This was way back in the early days of the Web—what we now romantically call Web 1.0. This was before Steve Jobs went back to Apple. Before Google. Before blogs, before Twitter, before Snapchat. And, before *social* anything.

Netscape was the browser of choice, and most people used a dial-up service to connect to the Internet through a desktop computer. At that time, there were only about 100,000 sites on the Internet (at the time, everyone called them *Web pages*). Two years later, there were more than 100 million; today there are over 700 million.

At the time, I was working for a fast-growing design firm. I had great clients and a terrific team—I felt as though I had reached a peak in my career. I was also teaching design classes in a new media program. Everyone was talking about a new economy driven by new technology. One of the classes I taught was on designing new systems that required technologies that seemed far off in the distant future. One, for instance, was a new, digital monetary system similar to today's bitcoin.

It was clear to me that there was a big wave coming. As a life-long surfer, I didn't know exactly what it was or where it was going but I knew I wanted to catch it. I convinced an engineer and another designer to start a little side project we called *Process1234*. We thought there might soon be a big need for established companies to develop new Web-based products and services, and we thought we could build a new consulting business around it. We tested the whole idea by doing a few jobs on the side—and it worked! We quit our jobs and took the leap into entrepreneurship.

Looking back, we had no idea what we were doing, but we were fueled by the belief that since we were designers, we could figure it out, and, once we did, we'd change the world.

Amazingly, Process1234 took off. It took fewer than six months to reach profitability and a solid business model. I then learned a lesson that many founders will understand: One of your first tasks in starting a new business should be to nail down your ceiling with your cofounders. That is, define what success looks like from the beginning. I wanted to scale our business to the moon; my ceiling was very high. However, one of my cofounders wanted to stay small. In the end, we just couldn't make it work, and shut Process1234 down, becoming part of that 90 percent failure statistic.

I learned a lot through that experience. What I didn't realize at the time was that, while we weren't able to scale Process1234, we had validated the need and the business model. As it turned out, we weren't alone. There were others who had the same idea, and my experience made me much more marketable than I would have been if I had stayed at my design job. Soon after, I moved to New York City, and joined what became the dotcom boom (and bust).

Every professional, company, and organization must learn how to continuously disrupt itself or someone else will.

There's an interesting scene midway through Walter Isaacson's masterful biography of Steve Jobs that crystallizes the need for change. It's 1997, shortly after Jobs returned to Apple after having been banished for a decade, and he's asking Mike Markkula, his mentor and original partner, for advice on getting the company back on track.

"Jobs's ambition was to build a company that would endure, and he asked Markkula what the formula for that would be," Isaacson writes. "Markkula replied that lasting companies know how to reinvent themselves. Hewlett-Packard had done that repeatedly; it started as an instrument company, then became a calculator company, then a computer company. 'Apple has been sidelined by Microsoft in the PC business,' Markkula said. 'You've got to reinvent the company to do some other thing, like other consumer products or devices. You've got to be like a butterfly and have a metamorphosis.' Jobs didn't say much, but he agreed."

We all know how that turned out. Apple's stock, which was selling for $13.25 the day that Guy Amelio, Apple's CEO between 1994 and 1997, was ousted, topped $700 a share in September 2012 under Jobs's leadership.

Agility is a must-have. And the great news is that any company can get smarter by using design to learn and adapt.

Failing Fast

There is a common phrase used in the startup community: *failing fast*. Go into any coworking space or early-stage startup office and you'll likely see it painted or posted on a wall.

Startups know very little about anything when they begin. They don't know their customer. They may have fuzzy ideas about the product or service around which they will build a company. Often, they don't even know the size of the market in which they will compete. There is simply no way to sit back and create a beautiful business plan, then execute it. They don't know what they don't know. They just have to start. They learn by doing.

Most startups also don't have the kind of resources big companies have in people, time, or money. They live in a world that could literally end tomorrow. They don't have the luxury of fearing failure. They must embrace it. In fact, they try to fail as quickly as possible so they can move on to the next thing—whatever that may be. *Failing fast* isn't just a catchy phrase. For most founders, it's a core value, an integral part of the whole lean startup method.

While this may sound foreign or even frightening for people who work in big companies, this kind of pressure isn't actually a bad thing. Whether you can see it or feel it, every company is facing a whole new level of complexity and risk of disruption. You might not feel the urgency yet, but you will.

Why not get ahead of it? Why not begin to get ready for what's coming?

You don't have to be in a startup to learn how to fail fast.

Any team or company can launch a new project, campaign, or initiative the way startups do. Learning what people need or want, building a prototype, measuring what worked and what didn't, then doing it all over again, are techniques that anyone can embrace.

While it may all sound new, the basic principles have been around for a long time.

One of my favorite stories is about Norm Larsen, the guy who designed and developed WD-40, the spray that stops doors from squeaking, cleans guitar strings, removes tomato stains from clothing, and has about a million other handy uses. What most people don't know is that WD-40 means Water Displacement, 40th formula..

The story goes that, in 1953, Norm needed to prevent rust and corrosion in nuclear missiles. He thought if he and his small team could create a product that could somehow remove or displace the water around the parts that created the rust, he could prevent corrosion. Norm failed thirty-nine times before he got it right. He finally cracked it on his fortieth try. As it turns out, the product he designed could do many other things and went on to become a huge success. Who knows how successful it might have been if he had stopped at attempt thirty-four!

Failing fast really means learning fast.

So, if you have a problem with the idea of failure, substitute the word *learn*, since failing faster essentially means learning faster. Each failure makes you smarter by helping you better understand what works and what doesn't.

While this concept is ingrained in the startup community, there's no getting around the fact that it's harder to embrace inside big companies. When a company reaches scale, success is all about planning and execution. The company's highest performers are invariably the managers who have the ability to create a good plan, then execute it with precision. Failure at that level generally isn't celebrated, since it's usually interpreted as bad planning or faulty execution. In a public company, with the constant pressure of quarterly results, it's difficult to celebrate failed projects, no matter how much may have been learned in the process.

Any company can make the shift from failing to learning fast through design.

Let's go back to the Golden Circle framework and revisit the *Why, How,* and *What.*

In the Designing for Agility approach, the *Why,* or purpose, is agility. The *How,* or process, is to learn, build, and measure. And the *What,* or product, we're designing, in this case, is Legos. Learn, build, measure is the same process used by most of today's startups and is at the heart of what Eric Reis and others have codified as *The Lean Startup method.*

We've talked about the *How*. Now let's talk about the *What*, and why it's important to think about your product or service like a big box of Legos.

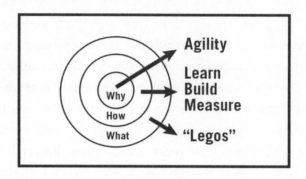

Legos not Lamborghinis

In chapter 1, we said the challenge for every company is to connect design with its growth strategy. This is what makes design *strategic*. So, when all is said and done, design is really all about growth—connecting the way a company designs to the way the company wants to grow. If a company has developed a product (or service) and it's ready to scale that product nationally or even globally, designing Lamborghinis—perfectly integrated systems is the only way to go.

And that is how The Coca-Cola Company scaled Coca-Cola for almost one hundred years, building Coke into an iconic, global, billion-dollar brand. As we discussed in chapter 2, the formula, the Spencerian script, the contour bottle, and the other elements have been critical to Coca-Cola's ability to scale.

But with the pivot in the company's business model toward being a total beverage company, it needed more. Coca-Cola still must design for scale but also must now design for agility. Its growth depends on leveraging a massive portfolio of products and brands, around the world, in different ways, all at the same time. This complexity, coupled with new external complexities, requires it to think differently about the stuff that's designed—communications, packaging, racks, coolers, trucks, supply chains, partnerships—all the things that drive the business. Like a startup, in many cases, the company doesn't fully know what consumers want or how a market may evolve; no one does. The only thing it knows is that things will change, and it needs a way to change with the market. The way it designs must help it learn and adapt.

I've traveled around the world and found one example that perfectly encapsulates how we need to think about design in fluid situations like these: Legos. From Beijing to Buenos Aires, everyone seems to know and love those sets of primary colored plastic bricks you played with as a kid.

Legos are more than just a toy for kids. Legos are a modular system.

Think about it. All the Lego bricks work together to help you make whatever you want to make—a wall, a house, a bridge, a starship. And the great thing is that they are designed so that it's super easy for a child to make something great. You don't have to know anything about physics or architecture or engineering to create a masterpiece.

Plus, they're easy to use right out of the box. You don't need a manual to tell you how they work. They come in just enough different colors and sizes to bring an idea to life, simply and intuitively. They can make anyone feel more creative. (True confession: I keep a set on my desk to help me get through long conference calls.)

In chapter 1, we said a system is a set of elements and behaviors that connect to do one thing. And in chapter 2, we talked a lot about *integrated* systems—systems that are designed (simplify, standardize, integrate) to be like a Lamborghini. This type of system works best when you want to scale. However, there's another kind of system that works best if you want to create agility.

> *Integrated systems help create scale; modular systems help create agility.*

Integrated systems are what you use when you're ready to scale. As a business, integrated systems help you reduce friction, keep your operating costs down, and keep your quality consistent.

Each element in an integrated system is designed to be unique and connect with other unique things in one way. Every piece, every part, every function is designed uniquely to fit together with the other pieces to create everything from a cold bottle of Coca-Cola to a timeless masterpiece like a Lamborghini.

Modular systems are different. Each element in a modular system is designed to be interchangeable and connect with other interchangeable elements in many different ways. This difference may sound small but it is actually quite big.

Modular systems, like Legos, allow you to learn by doing. They give you options. They let you learn and adapt on the fly. When you were a kid playing with Legos, if you didn't like how your house or castle or airplane was looking, it was quite easy to change it. In this massively volatile world, this is how we need to learn to design our products.

To see how this works, let's take a look at how a simple, modular system underpinned enormous creativity in an unexpected realm: musical jingles—songs attached to ads to make them memorable.

LESSON LEARNED #7

Get Out of the Building

At the Coca-Cola Company, as at many others, the people who are responsible for the operations of the business are in the field, not in corporate headquarters. This creates a natural tension when someone from the head office tries to convince someone in the field to try something new.

This dynamic is not unique to Coca-Cola. No matter who you are or what your title is, you can't just sit in your office and Skype or send emails to people in far-flung locales and expect change. If you're trying to create a big shift, you have to get out there and work together to make it happen.

There's a good reason for this: You probably don't know as much as you think you know. Most of us make this mistake (including me, of course). Until you get out there and actually see the problem, and meet the people who are trying to solve it, there's really no way to fully understand it. The actual experience of learning with people creates a trust that can't happen any other way. Talking about design is one thing, but actually applying what you know to a real scenario, live, with the people who are responsible for the business, is critical.

Startups get this. There's no way to design something that a lot of people want or need unless they get something quickly in front of a lot of people and test their assumptions. And once they do, they can rapidly change anything about the product based on actual data and results.

When you're trying to build a design-driven culture, you have to do the same thing. You have to find out how people are designing now, what they could be doing differently, and then—perhaps most important—how to incorporate all that in a language or set of tools that feels intuitive to them (not you).

So, no matter your experience, your title, or what you think you know, you've got to get out there and meet people, listen much more than talk, and adapt your way of thinking to the reality beyond your company's headquarters.

Key Takeaway: Get out there—get your idea out of your head or off a whiteboard and into people's hands as fast as possible. That's the only way to learn what you don't know about what you're building.

Coke Case: Five Notes

Michael Wolff, the founding partner of the international brand consulting firm Wolff Olins, once said, "A brand is a file in your mind—we put all of the attributes—the things we like about a product or company—in the file in our brain."

One of the most memorable things about the Coca-Cola brand is the music associated with it. The jingle "I'd Like to Buy the World a Coke," is lodged in millions of brain files around the globe. But for a patch of nasty weather, it might never have been written.

In January 1971, Bill Backer, the creative director on the Coca-Cola account for the advertising agency McCann-Erickson, was stranded by fog in an airport in Ireland. The weather forced an overnight stay and, by the next day, passengers were in a foul mood. Backer saw them gathered at a café, annoyed about their accommodations, but now laughing and sharing stories, snacks and bottles of Coke as they waited for the next flight out of town.

Becker scribbled: "I'd like to buy the world a Coke and keep it company," and tucked the napkin in his pocket.

Thinking back on it, he later wrote: "In that moment (I) saw a bottle of Coke in a whole new light . . . as more than a drink that refreshed a hundred million people a day in almost every corner of the globe. . . . The familiar words, 'Let's have a Coke,' were actually a subtle way of saying, 'Let's keep each other company for a while.'"

When Becker finally got to London, he sat down with songwriters to hammer out a melody to go with the words. The jingle, recorded by Australian pop group The New Seekers, was eventually used as the basis for a TV commercial shot in Rome, featuring one hundred young people from embassies and schools in the city. A full-length record based on the ad went on to become a Top 10 hit. The tune at its heart is consistently named one of the top advertising jingles of all time. "I'd like to buy the world a Coke" is arguably a *perfect* jingle—it's hard to image how it could have been designed any better.

In 2006, when Coca-Cola was making plans to launch Open Happiness, its first global advertising campaign in over a decade, it took a different approach. The campaign began with a film called *Happiness Factory*. It imagined the whimsical, animated world inside a Coca-Cola vending machine, complete with a cinematic soundscape.

That film presented the perfect opportunity to launch a new audio branding element. "We wanted the utility of music to give us instant recognition, global relevance, and consumer awareness. We wanted something that people would remember after the campaign stopped," said Jonathan Mildenhall, vice president, global advertising strategy at the time.

The company needed something that was independent of lyrics, that didn't require language to generate the recognition that the tune was linked to Coca-Cola.

Coca-Cola needed a modular, adaptable system— not a new jingle.

"The hook we were looking for could be found in the spine of the melody of the *Happiness Factory* score," says Nick Felder, Coca-Cola's global director of film and music production. After lots of trial and error, producers learned that the hook could be distilled into a fifteen-note melody, which was further tightened into a five-note mnemonic, a sort of "do do doo da do." When it was added to the soundtrack of the TV commercials, it instantly went viral, even though you couldn't, technically, sing it.

The team then tried remixing the tune with different beats, sounds, and rhythms. The goal was to see if the structure could easily adapt to different musical genres. They needed to create something that DJs, musicians, and agencies could share and make their own.

The really astonishing part of all this is that it really encompasses only three notes, since two repeat. Musicians were fascinated by the fragment, which is so highly restricted, yet so versatile.

The "Open Happiness" single, released in 2009, with Cee-Lo Green, Patrick Stump, Brendon Urie, and Janelle Monae was the first original song to include the melody. Some twenty-four versions were recorded in different languages and released in more than thirty countries.

A year after Coca-Cola created what it had begun calling the *Five Notes*, the company began planning for the FIFA World Cup in South Africa. Mildenhall suggested finding an African musician to interpret the Five Notes with big drums and a tribal beat.

As luck would have it, music executives had just discovered a young African singer with a song that had the potential to be the World Cup anthem he had been searching for.

K'naan is a young Somali singer who, as a boy, fled his war-torn homeland on one of the last commercial flights out of Mogadishu, then settled in Toronto with his family. There, the young rapper managed to get the attention of a record label, A&M Octone, which released his album, "Troubadour," in 2009. It included the song, "Wavin'

Flag," a sad, poetic tribute to the singer's native land, that has an up-beat chorus.

The music team thought it had potential, if K'naan was willing to adapt it to a celebration of soccer instead of a memory of Somalia. The singer was enthusiastic about the idea. "The Coke lyrics are the pop music side of me," he told Fast Company. "Creating a song you can hum at work."

The result was the "Wavin' Flag Celebration Mix," an anthem to the joys of being young and playing sports together.

Back in the studio, K'naan, delighted at the song's flexibility, re-corded eighteen different versions of the song, customized for differ-ent counties, with local musicians joining in a duet. "I find it exciting that ["Wavin' Flag" is] melodically acceptable in so many cultures, that it agrees with people's spirits in so many different places," he told *Billboard*.

The company was also delighted, since each version of the song in-cluded the Five Notes, a musical signature that made the song identifi-ably a collaboration with Coca-Cola. The simple structure of the song enabled musicians to create infinitely diverse and adaptable songs. Unlike "I'd Like to Buy the World a Coke," a Lamborghini of a song, the Five Notes are the Legos of music.

More Is More

Dieter Rams, head of design at Braun for over thirty years, once summed up his approach to design with the phrase "Weniger, aber besser" which translates as "Less, but better." Many of the products his team designed—coffee makers, calculators, radios, audio/visual equipment, consumer appliances, and office products—have found a permanent home in museums around the world, including MoMA in New York.

In the 1980s, Rams wrote a sort of manifesto called "10 Principles of Good Design." Many people call it the "10 Commandments of Design." If you read them, you'll quickly agree that Rams' principles are all relevant but most people stop at the surface, at how things look. They assume that so-called good design is about simple aesthetics; this is the disconnect for most business managers and design. They look at Rams' coffee machine from 1972 and their cut-throat market and scratch their head. They think, *"less is more" may work for coffee-makers but I sell real estate for a living. And have you seen the real estate market lately—total chaos.* It's very difficult to connect the notion that good design equals simple aesthetics for most companies.

In today's world, companies don't design to get into museums, they design to grow and remain relevant.

And this is a big problem in today's highly complex world—a marketplace filled with disruption and revolution. Design must connect to a company's growth strategy. And for most established companies, growth is all about agility.

For agility, less is actually *not* more—in fact, *more* is *more*. To adapt, we need more elements, more options, not fewer. We must use design to adapt—to figure out what works—to move quickly in rapidly changing conditions.

Look at the publishing world. You can now get most books in a variety of formats: hardcover, paperback, electronic, and audio. You can get sample chapters and short versions. You can get versions that let you read parts on a device of your choosing—an e-reader, a tablet, your phone—and then pick up where you left off to hear parts in audio format in the car on your way to work. You can buy your book in a store or online, from your easy chair, or from a WiFi-equipped plane at 33,000 feet. The publishing world is supplying all these options because consumers are demanding it. It gives a different spin to the old academic adage, "Publish or perish."

Every industry is in constant motion—revolutions are happening everywhere. Companies need more products, more services, more platforms, more suppliers, more partners, more channels, and more business models to adapt.

Look at the financial industry, the automotive industry, healthcare, and education. We live in a world where every company needs more options to remain relevant.

The Coca-Cola Company is acutely aware of this. As we noted earlier, most of what the company sells tastes better when it's cold. This is especially true for Coke itself. Earlier, we discussed *the perfect serve* and how it refers to a combination of the perfect product ingredients (the formula), the perfect glass (the contour bottle), and the perfect temperature (36 degrees Fahrenheit).

One of the biggest challenges for the company, especially in developing countries, is simply to keep Coke cold—not perfectly cold, just cold.

The company uses coolers to keep its products refrigerated. Nothing fancy, just a variation on what most people in developed countries have in their kitchens. A cooler is a cooler, right? Back in the early twentieth century it was. Coca-Cola partnered with the Glascock Brothers Manufacturing Company to design a cooler that could hold 72 bottles and 50 pounds of ice. It was basically a simple red box with the Coke logo on it. But it was quite effective and helped to scale the perfect serve around the world. Lots of people collect these; they remind us of an era frozen in time.

Today, things are quite different. The company doesn't have one hundred years of history to lean on in developing countries like China. Most people there have never even had a Coke or know that it tastes better when chilled. In fact, lots of people have never even heard of drinking a cold beverage. And since everything is new, there are no standards, no patterns, no formats for anything. That's a problem if the perfect way to enjoy your product is for it to be frosty.

In China, Coca-Cola had to learn by doing.

The company doesn't need one standardized cooler in China; it needs an adaptive system that can respond to very different and changing conditions. It needs little ones, medium ones, and big ones. It needs low-cost ones and premium ones. It needs coolers that are easy to service and ones that can essentially service themselves. It needs coolers that can manage different types of electricity. It needs coolers that it can brand Coca-Cola, Sprite, Minute Maid, or VitaminWater, depending on what the shopkeeper wants to feature. The bottom line is, the company doesn't need one perfect cooler—a Lamborghini. It needs a box of Legos—an adaptive system it can use to design different kinds of coolers that can flex to different conditions.

This approach itself is infinitely flexible. The company has used it to design everything from musical signatures to coolers to its distribution systems.

Coke Case: Manual Distribution Centers

In most developed countries, it's quite common to see our big red Coca-Cola trucks delivering products to retailers from little mom-and-pop stores to giant Walmart Supercenters. As you can imagine, the company's drivers have this down to a science. Every turn is accounted for—they work with clockwork precision. This is how Coca-Cola maintains its leadership through a relentless focus on execution.

However, in places like Dar es Salaam, Tanzania, and Addis Ababa, Ethiopia, the streets are often very narrow dirt roads, without the infrastructure developed countries take for granted. And the shops are small, with limited access, electricity, and security. Using a big red truck is more than impractical, it's impossible.

Why does this matter? Ethiopia, Kenya, Nigeria: Places like these are the future for Coca-Cola. For the first time in their lives, people living in developing countries in Africa as well as similar countries in Latin America and Asia have more opportunities than they have ever had. For the first time, they can afford to buy things beyond necessities, like a television, a cell phone, or a Coke. To meet this new demand, the company can't apply the same approach it's used in developed countries. It has to design its business to adapt to very dynamic conditions.

In 1999, Coca-Cola Sabco (CCS), the company's South African bottling partner, designed a program—a modular system—to tackle this problem in Ethiopia. It created ten Manual Distribution Centers (MDCs) as a prototype for testing whether individual entrepreneurs could be enlisted as small-scale distributors. The idea was that these entrepreneurs would hire employees to use pushcarts and bicycles to deliver product to the small restaurants, bars, corner stores, and one-person kiosks in their neighborhood.

Before recruiting distributors, Coca-Cola Sabco collected data on all the retail outlets in a target area. Typically, each MDC site would be about one kilometer in circumference with a maximum of one hundred fifty retail outlets. By keeping the area small, but economically vibrant enough to ensure a new distributor of a reasonable profit, CCS made sure that business conditions for a new owner were stacked toward success. Still, it was important for the company to understand how each of the channels would function and operate in each market. One size definitely did not fit all.

The MDC distributors that CCS enlisted were mostly first-time business owners with limited education. They were vetted for their willingness to work full time, their strong work ethic, their access to a site suitable for product warehousing, and their ability to raise the capital to finance their new business.

The most critical factor in their success is regular training. The new recruits need to be coached in things like basic business skills, account development, merchandising and customer service, and warehouse and distribution management. Then, they would need follow-up guidance to expand and manage their growing businesses.

The company used lots of feedback loops to learn.

It is also critical to be able to reassess how things are working on a regular basis, using lots of feedback loops, since market conditions in emerging countries change rapidly. Without constant feedback, the company wouldn't be able to adjust.

By 2002, CCS had expanded the program throughout its markets in East Africa. Today, there are more than 2,500 MDCs in Africa, employing over 12,000 people.

This system has been a success on a variety of levels. It certainly helped Coca-Cola solve a complex distribution problem. For example, the MDCs provide retailers with frequent small deliveries of products, something the company couldn't do with big trucks (even if the road conditions allowed), since the shops are often so small that they don't have storage for a week's worth of products and would otherwise run out. In Ethiopia and Tanzania, more than 80 percent of Coca-Cola's volume is now distributed through MDCs. In Kenya and Uganda that number is even higher: 90 and 99 percent, respectively.

Keep in mind that for Coca-Cola, MDC is a very modular system—it's designed to flex to the local market conditions.

In some cases, an MDC's employees will deliver by bicycle. In other cases, they deliver by a small boat down a river. In other cases it's by donkey or camel—whatever it takes to get the job done.

It's also created lots of new jobs, especially for women. These small businesses are fueling a growing middle class, as well as enhancing the owners' long-term employability by teaching valuable skills. Even if an MDC owner should decide to move on to another business, he or she would likely then have the economic resources to be a customer of our products. Talk about a win-win for adaptability!

Designing for agility requires designing modular, adaptive systems—but that's not all—you have to learn to plan backward.

LESSON LEARNED #8

Plan Backward

If you're in a leadership position at a big company, chances are you're good at planning for the future. For most leaders, their business plan is the roadmap, the thing that gives direction to their team and allows them to measure success. Business plans are critical, especially for large-scale companies.

The next time you're in a position to make a plan, try something new: Plan backward. Try getting results first, then plan around them. This is the thing that *lean* start-ups do best. Before they spend a lot of money, commit to a big deal, or hire a bunch of people, they get some real, tangible results—sales, users, and so on—then plan based on what actually happened.

Marketing guru Jim Ewel blogged, "Too many traditional marketers plan big campaigns, spend big bucks, only to search at the end for favorable data to justify all that money spent."

Sound familiar?

Next time, determine who your target customers are and the key assumptions you have about them—then brainstorm a few quick, low-cost experiments to test your assumptions. Find out what those customers *really* think, what they will *really* buy, and how much they will *really* pay for your product or service. Then iterate—react to what you learned and try it again.

After you've got those results in front of you, sit down and make a plan. You will benefit from having done a few experiments, while spending little of your budget. Take what you've learned, then plan, design, execute—based on what you now know will work.

Key Takeaway: Get results—*then* plan.

Shark-Bite Problems

Every time I sit down on a plane, I can guess what's coming. The exchange usually goes something like this . . .

"Hi, I'm David. What's your name?"

"Tim."

"Nice to meet you, Tim. First time to Jakarta?"

"Yep, first time. What do you do, Dave?"

"I work for Coca-Cola"

"Oh, really? I'm sure you get this all the time, but I've always had an idea for you guys. You should really think about making a . . ."

I've heard many, many ideas this way. Ideas also sometimes show up unexpectedly. I've often come back to my hotel room to find an idea—a packaging prototype, a sketch, and so on, usually with a very nice note attached, from someone who probably bribed the cleaning staff to get it in my room.

All of these efforts have one thing in common. They aren't actually ideas, they're *solutions*—solutions to problems that haven't been validated. And while the solution may look cool or seem to be very innovative, that doesn't mean it solves a problem or that anyone will actually want to buy it.

This happens a lot inside big companies. Someone falls in love with a solution and then tries to find a way to get it funded or somehow supported by senior management.

The problem with this approach is the solution (invariably described as a "big idea") may only solve a tiny problem or only meet the need of a very small set of people. Meaning, there's a good chance that the company may spend more in designing, manufacturing, and selling the thing than they can actually make. And that's not a good thing. This is how many pet projects create black holes of wasted time, energy, and money inside big companies.

Startups don't work this way. They don't have the luxury to do so. Rather than spend a lot of effort on a solution, startups spend time on the actual problem—learning as much as they can before they begin to create a solution.

One common way they do this is to figure out the amount of pain the problem creates for people. Is it a mosquito-bite level of pain or a shark-bite level of pain? The bigger the pain, the bigger the gain.

This was exactly the approach Coca-Cola used to figure out what was needed when it began designing a retail merchandising system in Latin America. Let's go to Colombia and see what the company learned.

Coke Case: XMod Retail Design System

The Chapinero neighborhood in Bogota is just like thousands of other neighborhoods across Latin America. It's filled with tiny stores that function as neighborhood dispensaries of everything from produce to housewares, and are essential social centers of the community, where gossip is exchanged along with the day's vegetables.

These stores generally measure no more than a few square meters, and often are side-by-side with similar stores. Their differences, however, are readily apparent to their customers. At one shop, for example, they can find everything they need for breakfast, while the store next door peddles staples for an evening meal, along with a side order of neighborhood news.

While each of these shops individually generates miniscule revenues compared with, say, a Walmart or Carrefour, in the aggregate they represent Coca-Cola's biggest sales channel in Latin America.

"There are 3.5 million mom-and-pop shops across Latin America, which generate more than half of our sales," says Rodolfo E. Salas, Coca-Cola Latin America's vice president of Customer and Commercial Development at the time. Another large percentage of our sales comes from independent restaurants, and 10 to 15 percent originate everywhere else, from McDonald's to superstores. Compare that to our business in the United States or Europe, where fast-food chains, giant box stores, and supermarkets account for the vast majority of our sales.

Because of the market's size, and potential, the company recognized that if it could help a small retailer maximize sales in his or her tiny space, it would be a win-win for both sides. Trouble was that, in the past, the company was less successful than it had hoped.

"We tried different approaches fourteen times," says Alba Adamo, the group director of marketing for Latin America. There are twenty-one countries in Latin America. That made for a cacophony of ideas as to how best to reach this market.

For example, years ago, Coca-Cola designed beautiful shelving units to fit near the cash register. Designers thought they'd help a shop owner sell a last-minute can of Coke or Fanta. However, shopkeepers kept moving them because they got in the way of conversations with their customers. Keeping a personal connection to shoppers is critical—it's what keeps them relevant in their community.

In another case, designers created what they thought was terrific framing for point-of-purchase displays that would make a retailer's top shelf look clean and Coca-Cola's products pop. That didn't work either. Store owners complained that the signage took up valuable storage space for boxes of merchandise, an important consideration where every millimeter counts.

The problem was that designers had created all of these examples in isolation, in silos—each as stand-alone projects with their own teams. This approach to design is quite common especially in big companies.

It was clear that the company needed an approach that was comprehensive, flexible enough to address different stores' merchandise selections, adaptable to the many shapes and sizes of shops, and, above all, sensitive to the ultimate consumers—the shopkeepers and their customers.

These projects also had to be responsive to the entire ecosystem of the trade. "The shopper is attended by the shopkeeper, who is serviced by the merchandiser, who is supported by the sales developer, who may or may not have anything to do with the truck driver," says Gerardo Garcia, Coca-Cola's global group design director. And, of course, they had to work for the Coca-Cola bottlers, who are its primary partners in any country.

In addition, Coca-Cola had a rather urgent need of its own: As its portfolio of brands increased, from the traditional Coca-Cola, Sprite, and Fanta, to teas, waters, energy drinks, juices, and more, it needed to find a way to help shopkeepers display its new products in the same small footprint.

The problem was threefold: These diminutive stores tended to be cluttered, with no visible order to the merchandise; they were easy to miss, since they were crammed into small nooks and crannies in the neighborhood; and, once inside, they were hard to navigate, with intense competition among products for very little space.

In 2009, the company set out to create a modular system of elements, what it called the *XMod Retail Design System*, comprising racks, counter displays, coolers, and frames for signage, which would encompass all those needs.

The company's Latin American team was determined to really understand the markets at a very granular level. Researchers did dozens of walk-arounds with our local sales force, some of whom visit sixty to eighty stores per day. The goal was to see what a typical shopkeeper's day looked like. They discovered, for example, that a proprietor of a breakfast shop rises at three in the morning to start baking bread. By five, she's opening her doors, and her business is brisk through noon.

By contrast, a shop in the downtown area has a very different traffic pattern. His business is less about leisurely conversation than about speedy transactions: a snack on the way to work, a sandwich and a Coke at lunch, a pack of batteries, a pack of gum, a pack of cigarettes. He needs efficiency, a way to help him wait on four people at once.

This was a critical step.

People say one thing and do another. The company couldn't learn what the real needs were through focus groups or by hiring some smart consultants—it had to watch what people really did, to find out what was really going on.

The goal was to capture all of the needs from each stakeholder's perspective. This was the only way the company could create the shared value necessary for this to be successful.

Researchers began to learn how customers shopped. Unlike the United States, where a shopper might load up a grocery cart with all the supplies she needs once a week, many people in countries like Mexico shop daily and sometimes as much as three times a day. The company needed to understand the solutions they were looking for: What's for breakfast or lunch? What can I make for dinner if I have very little to spend?

The proprietor of a shop in Latin America is called a *tendero*. Making his or her life easier became another focus.

"If a *tendero* did not see a clear functionality for an asset, it was taken out," says Erika Gomez, one of lead designers of the XMod System. "If it was pure advertisement for us, it had to go."

The modular elements designed for these shops could be configured in different ways that adapted to a shop's dimensions. One of the most popular pieces, for example, was a rack that could be as short as one meter, with two shelves, or as tall as two meters, with four to five shelves. Several could be put side-by-side to form a horizontal wall, or they could flank a cooler. Smaller ones could be outfitted with wheels to serve as carts.

In addition, the units needed to be able to be installed quickly and easily. "The barrier is speed," says Salas. "Downtime for a shop owner is money out of his pocket." In the past, units came from the factory, preassembled. For this project, designers took a page from Ikea, and crafted them so that they could be packed flat.

In the initial round of installations, planners determined the time of day or night during which a particular store would be least busy, and tried to accommodate store owners' concerns for disruption and lost business.

The company has no illusions that the system it's developed is its final version. The ability to iterate, and build upon the pieces, is one of its most important aspects.

"One of our objectives was to make it and fix it as we go," says Gomez. "Not to make it perfect from the beginning."

From a brand standpoint, the color selection of assets was designed to help to facilitate navigation of a store for a customer. Red, for example, is the signature color of Coca-Cola, so a customer seeking a sparkling beverage would know that it would likely be found in a red cooler. Green is the color associated with juice brands, and blue signals water brands.

Researchers learned that in Latin America, where fresh fruit is plentiful and cheap, it's hazardous to use materials that might be perceived as artificial or inauthentic. This was particularly important with regard to the juice business, since the company wanted shoppers to see the connection between its juice and the grove where it originated. That meant that when designers wanted to use wood, it had to be *real* wood, not wood-printed paper, glued on a backing. Wood, of course, is expensive, but they found that white pine—a cheaper wood—was as effective, or more so, than, say, a beautifully tooled oak.

"It doesn't have to be fancy," says Garcia. "Actually, if it's not perfect it's even better, because we're trying to communicate that it came from the grove, and that it's authentic."

The rollout of the system began in Colombia in early 2012 with five hundred stores, and the early returns were good. "We got an initial lift of twenty-five percent, that eventually settled down to fifteen percent, and remained stable," says Salas. But the best thing, Salas says, has been to see a store owner filled with pride at her newly configured space, and to watch with her as her business grows.

The beauty of the system is that it will constantly evolve as the company learns what works and what doesn't, what retailers find most useful, what their customers most respond to, how the company's own portfolio of products changes, and how the general retail landscape shifts within each country. What's more, it can be adapted to different geographies, and their particular needs, as well as to different price points, as Coca-Cola looks to develop this system internationally.

First, Get Smarter

In short: Every company is at risk of having a Kodak moment. These days, companies must learn how to continuously disrupt themselves or someone else will. But how?

It only happens by design. The way you design your products, your relationships, your operations, and your organization can help you learn and adapt. Most of the issues that companies face today are not only complicated, but connected. However, any company can design for the agility that it needs to fail fast, adapt to constantly changing conditions, and remain relevant.

The fundamental difference in designing for agility is that you need to think about many solutions to many problems simultaneously. This goes against our natural inclination to think that there's one right answer, one elegant solution, which will adapt to all situations.

Thinking like this is messy. There's no way to know all the things that you don't know that will require a last-minute change in plans, or modification of your strategy. There's no way to predict the macroeconomic environment in which your business will operate, the vagaries of the weather and its impact on your company's sales, political upheaval, social media frenzy, or random acts of lunacy that somehow affect your business. Understanding that need for flexibility, allowing for continuous iteration—indeed, being constantly open to better ideas or solutions as they present themselves—is a powerful way by which to stay ahead of the game and keep your business viable and ahead of the competition.

CHAPTER 5

Faster

"For the things we have to learn before we can do them,
we learn by doing them."

Aristotle

I t was Thursday, during my first week at Coca-Cola, when I was invited to join one of our global marketing teams for a meeting. The team was responsible for Fanta's global growth strategy. I didn't know much about Fanta, but figured this might be my first chance to dig into one of the company's biggest global brands. I had been a designer, an entrepreneur, a consultant, and a professor, but this was my first corporate job. I didn't really know what to expect, but I was pumped.

Walking into a giant, windowless conference room, I glanced at about a hundred different packaging images on the wall. I shook a bunch of hands, and found my seat at a big, glossy table. No sooner had I sat down than everyone turned in my direction, clearly expecting me to say something.

"Okay," I asked, "what do we do now?"

The marketing VP turned to me as if the task were perfectly obvious: "You're the new packaging guy, right? Pick one. "

"Pick one what?" I asked, hoping he wasn't really asking what I thought he was.

"Pick a new label for us to roll out globally."

Now, I wasn't sure if he was joking or really meant it but, for a moment, I felt like I was in the middle of an art contest. I don't think I was wearing black, but I felt like I should have been, and maybe even a beret, like some sort of senior-level art critic. I had zero context. I knew nothing about the brand strategy, the brand's portfolio, the consumer, the retailers, the competitive issues, the brand equities, or any of our operational constraints. *This* was exactly what I had been afraid of. A thought flickered through my brain: "Maybe I made the wrong decision. Maybe it isn't too late to turn in my badge. Maybe if I slip out now, no one will notice."

I knew our marketing guy wasn't just being flippant. However, at that time, I didn't realize just how big an opportunity we had to create more value through design. I knew we had to think about design differently. *Design* had to be bigger than a label, a package, or even a brand. We had a long way to go, but we had to start somewhere. I also knew that I had a lot to learn about the business. So I took a deep breath and plunged in:

"How many countries sell Fanta?" I asked.

"One hundred eighty."

"How many flavors?"

"Over one hundred."

"How many different sizes of packages do we sell?"

"A lot—it's different in every country."

"How consistent is the brand's identity around the world?"

"It's fractured and we need to fix it."

"How important is this brand to our portfolio?"

"It's second only to Coke in global sales."

"What kinds of channels do we sell it in?"

"Anything from a vending machine in North America to a big-box retailer in Europe to a mom-and-pop in Brazil."

By the end of this back and forth, the problem was clear. "We don't need a label," I said, "we need a new system—a *modular* system that can adapt to different needs all around the world. And the good news is, we can design that."

This might not sound like a big deal now, but it certainly was then. This was to be the beginning of a new approach to design for The Coca-Cola Company. We had used a Designing for Scale approach to grow Coca-Cola into a billion-dollar brand. Now we needed to design for agility.

In chapter 4, we used the Golden Circle to show the *Why, How,* and *What* of our approach.

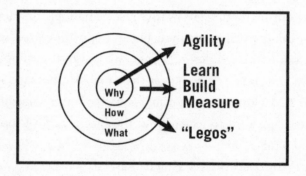

In this chapter, we're going to focus on speed, how Designing for Agility can actually help companies adapt faster to changing conditions.

In the last chapter, we introduced the concept of modular systems with an example that everyone understands—Legos. We said that Legos (modular systems) help you learn and adapt. Building or developing your product using this process is different than developing integrated products—Lamborghinis—largely because it can give you more speed. And that's a good thing whether you're part of a large organization managing your scale, or part of a startup fighting for survival. Moving as fast as, or faster than, your closest competitor is the name of the game.

Let's go back and look at Legos to connect this idea of designing modular systems and speed.

Built for Speed

Legos are a beautiful system but, more important, they're a *modular* system. It's easy to understand why.

There are two things that make Legos modular.

First of all, Legos have *fixed* and *flexible* elements. Among the fixed elements are color and shape. I remember, when I was a kid, you could only buy the basic set—four to five different shapes—in white, red, yellow, black, and blue. Their material—plastic—is also fixed. You'll never see Legos made of wood or metal or any other material. This helps Lego manage a global supply chain and maintain consistency and quality across its manufacturing and fulfillment processes.

In addition, all Legos connect in the same way, with little round studs on top that snap into holes on another brick's bottom. They're super easy. This is what makes the whole system of bricks modular—each brick, no matter what size or color, connects with the other ones quickly.

Over the years, Lego has introduced many different kinds of sets, keeping pace with kids' boundless imaginations. These are the *flexible elements* that create the adaptability that has helped Legos stay relevant for generations.

Designing this way, with both fixed and flexible elements, has created agility for Lego. The company is able to easily create, delete, or combine various elements to introduce new sets into the marketplace based on changing consumer behavior. Now, if you want to use Legos to build skyscrapers worthy of a Shanghai skyline, complicated Death Stars, pteranodon dinosaurs, or Hobbit huts, Legos has a set for you.

Now what if you could design Lego-like systems for your company? What if you could design your products, your factories, your supply chain, your marketing campaigns and even your strategies to be modular systems? Imagine that you could add a new feature or quickly swap a component or bolt on a new acquisition as quickly as you used to add a few bricks to your Lego house when you were a kid. That's the power of designing this way as a company.

Pivot, Persevere, or Die

In chapter 2, we talked about designing perfectly integrated products. Doing this by simplifying, standardizing, and integrating a product is a traditional way of doing business for big companies. But this strategy is inadequate in a world that is changing faster than they are. No one understands uncertainty better than startups. Let's look at the reasons for this.

Steve Blank, entrepreneur, professor, and author of *Four Steps to the Epiphany* and *The Startup Owner's Manual*, is widely recognized as the founder of the *Lean Startup* revolution.

Blank was the first to codify the definition of a startup that we mentioned in the beginning of this section of the book: "A startup is an organization formed to search for a repeatable and scalable business model."

Startups *survive* on speed. Unlike established companies, startups typically adjust and change almost daily. Contrast that with some big companies, where it can take a month just to get the right cross-functional team together for a project kickoff meeting. Many startups would be dead before the month was over if they moved that slowly.

The startups that ultimately make it are masters of a maneuver that *The Lean Startup* author Eric Reis calls *the pivot*.

Pivoting is when a company abruptly changes its strategy, altering a fundamental part of its business model, without changing its vision.

Often this is the result of testing various hypotheses or assumptions on real users. Without a pivot, Twitter might still be trying to make a success of audio podcasting, YouTube would have been a video-dating site, and Groupon would have continued organizing political protests.

When startups pivot, the course correction may be slight or radical, but the key is speed. As soon as it's clear that their model isn't working the founders change direction, *quickly*. This could be after a week, or maybe a month or two, but generally not much more than that. If the goal of all startups is to create a viable and sustainable business model that can scale, any piece of the model may need to pivot if it begins to slow down—the product, the customer, the whole value proposition itself—as well as the profit model, or the manufacturing/distribution model. The product may need a new feature, the sales channel may be wrong, or the marketing strategy may be ineffective. Everything is open for discussion; nothing is precious—we're talking life or death.

Paul Graham, Y Combinator cofounder, calls this willingness to change direction "fluidity of mind," and, he says, it's an essential character trait of successful entrepreneurs. Instead of holding on to an idea out of sheer stubbornness or because one's ego is tied up in being right, successful entrepreneurs are willing to reframe what they see and adapt on the fly.

These entrepreneurs are experts in *systems thinking* (understanding how systems work and how to design solutions to problems using systems). They may not even know it but, to be successful, they must constantly be thinking and designing their startup as a modular system. The way they design their product, their marketing strategy, or their partnerships must be in a way in which they can add or eliminate pieces quickly as they iterate on their business model.

Modular products or services enable companies to pivot faster.

But you don't need to be a startup to use this tactic. Let's look at a Coca-Cola project that used this approach to design a new modular system for one of its fastest-growing categories: juice.

Coke Case: Global Juice Visual Identity System

Designing a visual identity system for one of the world's biggest brands, like Coke, is a daunting task, but, in many ways, it's easier than designing a visual identity system for a portfolio of brands.

Why?

A brand's visual identity system has to do two things. First, it must translate the brand's emotional connection to people. Second, it must connect with the product's rational attributes, creating a unique identity for the brand. Then, art directors, designers, and brand managers can use the visual identity system to brand everything from packaging to advertising to the retail experience.

For example, when we redesigned the visual identity system for Coke, we had to connect the emotional idea of Open Happiness with the product's attributes—the refreshing taste, bubbles, and distinctive flavor, while also leveraging the decades of equity built in things like the Spencerian script. We created a very *integrated* system. As in a Lamborghini, every element was locked down.

Not so with juice.

"We taste fruit with our eyes," says Coca-Cola design director Tom Farrell.

Therein lies a problem. You may not realize it, but your perception of what an orange should look like is intimately connected with where you live. For a company looking to connect with a shopper in the juice aisle, those subtle differences can make the difference between a global hit and a market failure.

Back in 2008, the company was in the midst of acquiring a variety of smaller juice brands around the world, each with its own brand strategy, identity, packaging, and communications.

Juice represents an important category for the company; it has more than one hundred juice brands worldwide, in 145 countries, and growing its juice portfolio was critical to its growth strategy.

The company needed a visual identity system (VIS) that could provide a common look and feel across its juice portfolio. To do that, it needed a modular system that would give it the flexibility and speed it needed to add (or delete) various brands and products as it tried to capture maximum share of the juice market.

We knew we had a big job ahead of us, but we had yet to realize just how daunting a task we faced until we gathered all our products into one room and started to look at the problem. There was Cappy, a hugely popular brand in Central and Eastern Europe, and Del Valle and Andina, brands which dominate in Central and South America. Minute Maid, of course, in North America. And Minute Maid Pulpy Super Milky, an important brand in China. And those were just the big ones.

"It was very scary," says Farrell. "It was chaos. There was a redundancy of logos, colors, fonts, shapes, and sizes. There wasn't any sort of logic connecting these elements together."

That was no surprise. Through lots of mergers and acquisitions, as well as organic development, the company had built up a portfolio of dozens of juice brands. Even though the growth process made sense, the result was a cacophony of different looks and styles.

To get clarification of the problem, we knew we needed to see what shoppers saw: How all the company's various juice products competed on a shelf with their closest competitors. So, we simulated typical shelf sets from around the world and began to document the obvious things that needed to be fixed, and things that simply needed more exploration.

This is when it became very clear that the company had a massive opportunity to create much more efficiency across its portfolio, as well as a chance to be much more effective.

In addition to creating a common look and feel for Coca-Cola's juice brands, we knew we'd also have to build in a way to accommodate the subtle but critical cultural differences in fruit preferences that had the potential to make or break it in far-flung markets. We needed to capture the exact orange that the Chinese see in their mind's eye, the perfect orange that would resonate for the Brazilians, and the quintessential orange that the French would find authentic. Not to mention the lemon, the mango, the peach, the grape, and the guava. And we needed to do it *fast*.

We needed a solution that could adapt from Beijing to Buenos Aires.

From our research, we knew that the packaging needed to reflect the actual fruit inside with visceral resonance. Then it hit us: "The one core truth around Coca-Cola's juice business is that the company is in it from grove to glass," says Farrell. "It owns the farms. It partners with the growers. It doesn't buy juice on the open market. So this notion that it's connected to the land is fundamental."

How do you translate that into a brand's identity? What does "from grove to glass" look like? Do you use an image of a farmer? How about the grove? We tried all these, constantly iterating, getting feedback, making subtle shifts, then big ones, and vice versa.

We finally landed on a very deliberate presentation of the fruit. "We wanted to create, for the consumer, a sense of familiarity," says Farrell. "The idea that this is uncannily like something they've seen before." The subtle mnemonic that ties the display together is that slice of fruit on top, which looks like a smile.

We knew we were on to something when one person in our test group, looking at the cartons lined up next to each other in the refrigerator case, said, "Oh, it looks like the produce aisle."

Still, we weren't done. While we had resolved the issue of product imagery, we needed to solve other major elements: the information architecture (the flavor, the nutritional information) and the brand identity itself.

Years ago, Farrell was sitting at the theater watching *The Nutcracker*, when he noticed that the curtains never closed. He saw that the main elements were always onstage, but the set designers relied on modular elements to seamlessly change the staging.

That seamless modularity is not so different, he realized, from creating a template for a bottle of juice. "Your fruits, your operatic heroes, Clara, the Nutcracker, are up front," says Farrell. They change based on local tastes. And your category cue—green for juice, blue for refreshment drinks like water—changes as well. But the nutritional information remains fixed, except for differences in language.

A global visual identity is a fixed-flexible model. "The skeleton is the same, but we can hang different clothes on it," says Farrell. Local marketers amplify the pieces that resonate in their regions, while the design's DNA remains recognizable worldwide.

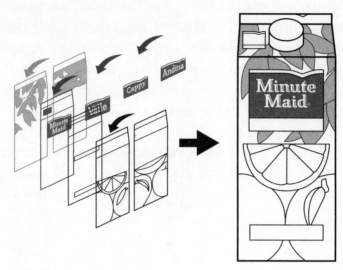

Copyright, The Coca-Cola Company

Take the Minute Maid logo, with its black rectangle, white text, and green horizon line that appears above. That green line acts as a metaphor for the company's deep connection to the land, and it stays the same across all packages.

We iterated many, many times to come up with the final version of the logo, trying many different lines, different blacks, and typefaces.

We used the same process for the other elements—lots of iteration but the whole point was to design a box of Legos: a set of fixed and flexible elements that we could mix and match depending on our needs around the world

The Global Juice Visual Identity System we created had three parts: the brand identity elements (fixed and flexible), the information architecture (the logic), and the standards (the rules) for how everything connected to one another. Together, they created a consistent, or common, look and feel across the portfolio. And because we had designed a modular system, we could pivot faster than before.

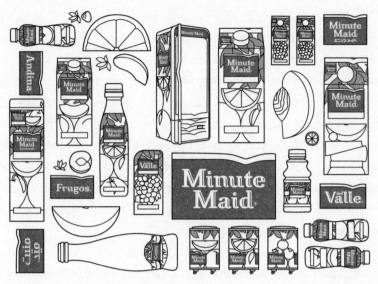

Copyright, The Coca-Cola Company

Learning by Doing

As you can see, designing modular systems is often messy—there's nothing predictable about it. There is constant change as the team struggles to get to a solution that works.

As we discussed earlier, *prototyping*—rapidly visualizing or making a model of an idea—is a powerful way of getting the concept out of your head and onto the table for everyone to see, poke at, and build on. You don't have to know how to draw, or be particularly adept at crafts, to do this. Anyone can. And almost anything can be used: markers, paper, tape, toothpicks, Post-it notes, whatever is close at hand.

Prototyping is fundamental at Stanford's d.school—it's one of the four pillars of its D.Manifesto (all you need to know on the back of a napkin).

"At the d.school, we learn by doing," the d.school notes in its Web site. "We don't just ask our students to solve a problem, we ask them to define what the problem is. Students start in the field, where they develop empathy for people they design for, uncovering real human needs they want to address. They then iterate to develop an unexpected range of possible solutions, and create rough prototypes to take back out into the field and test with real people. Our bias is toward action, followed by reflection on personal discoveries about process. Experience is measured by iteration: students run through as many cycles as they possibly can on any project. Each cycle brings stronger insights and more unexpected solutions."

Prototyping is critical for most startups as well. Walk into any co-working space in the world and you'll see whiteboards, Post-it notes, and Sharpies, the classic tools for visualizing an idea.

Prototypes exist to help you learn faster.

The key to prototypes—from a simple sketch to a robust working model—is learning. They exist to help the company figure out, as quickly as possible, what works and what doesn't. This creates agility—the flexibility needed to quickly pivot or adapt to rapidly changing conditions.

At Coca-Cola, prototyping is critical. Things are changing so fast the company simply doesn't know what it doesn't know, and it relies on prototyping to help it learn by doing. This applies to stuff that it's done in the past as well as things that are new—like farming mangos.

LESSON LEARNED #9

Visualize Your Idea

When your business card says "designer" and "Coca-Cola," conversation with new acquaintances invariably goes in one of two directions—design or Coke. When we go down the design path, nine times out of ten, my new friend says something like, "I could never be a designer. I was never good at drawing or painting." And it always startles them when I say, "Yeah, me neither."

So, it may seem counterintuitive to say that the first step in the design process is to learn how to visualize your ideas. If you can get the idea out of your head and onto a piece of paper, whiteboard, or tablet, more people will be able to understand it, build on it, and move it forward. And you don't have to take an art class to visualize your idea. You just have to make it visible.

Your sketch can be as crude as a first grader's drawing; the point is not artistic excellence, but simply a way of starting a discussion around a tangible idea.

You don't need a lab or a special room for this, but you do need enough space and a few tools to encourage collaboration.

At Coca-Cola, any time we need to discuss an idea, we make sure there's a whiteboard and some Post-it notes close by. Just having these things within arm's reach makes it easy for someone to jump up and begin visualizing an idea.

Key Takeaway: Don't let inhibitions about artistic talent, or lack of it, stop you from sketching your idea. The point is not to rival Picasso; it's to get your idea into a form whereby others can begin discussing it.

Coke Case: Project Unnati

India is one of the world's top mango producers, growing 55 percent of the globe's crops. That's important to Coca-Cola because it needs a lot of mangoes in South Asia. Indians go wild for a brand of mango juice we sell called Maaza. It accounts for nearly 70 percent of the market and, in a country of 1.2 billion, that's a big market.

That's the good news. The bad news is that to keep up with the growing demand, the company needed to figure out how to get more mangoes—fast.

It began by looking for the shark-bite problem. In India, the problem is a lot of people own land but don't have the tools or skills to farm the land effectively.

In South Africa, farmers pioneered a technique called *high-density cultivation*. Essentially, it involves planting crops very close together, and pruning them aggressively to force them to yield more fruit in less space. It's sort of like growing bonsai trees. Several years ago, Indian agricultural officials, on a tour of the South African plantations, heard about the method and were impressed. They resolved to give it a try back home with the mango crop.

A conventional mango grove features about forty trees per acre. Traditionally, they're allowed to grow tall, with expansive canopies. It generally takes between seven and nine years for a tree to reach the point at which it produces enough fruit to make money for its farmer.

Initially, the Indian government tried planting two hundred trees per acre. The results were promising, and encouraged them to try even harder.

Since Coca-Cola needed a lot of mangoes, the company thought it might be able to help make a bigger impact and, in the process, help a lot more farmers benefit from bigger yields per acre. That would be good for the farmers, and good for India's GDP, and it would provide the mangoes Coca-Cola needed to keep up with demand.

*But what did Coca-Cola know about farming,
specifically, high-density farming? There was only
one way for it to find out: Learn by doing.*

Coca-Cola's team in India partnered with Jain Irrigation on an ambitious $2 million pilot project: six hundred trees per acre in Andhra
Pradesh's Chittoor district, a region famous for its mango production.

The goal was to establish one hundred demonstration farms over
the next five years and to train an estimated fifty thousand mango
farmers in the technique. The program, Project Unnati, uses specially
designed buses to provide on-the-job training.

The farmers learn how to plant the trees close together, and to
prune their canopies to allow the most light to reach lower branches,
while never letting them get taller than seven feet high. That's the maximum height at which a farmer can pick his crop manually, without
having to invest in either expensive equipment or other laborers. As a
consequence, each farmer's own profit is maximized.

The mango university also teaches sustainable drip irrigation meth-
ods for conserving precious water.

It's estimated that using the new technique will double crop yields,
with trees reaching their full potential in only three to four years.

*Speed is the key—more fruit, more juice, more market
share—good for the farmers and good for the company.*

This sounds like a great end-to-end story but, like most things, it
didn't go off without a few hitches. The company learned a lot along

the way, making lots of mistakes, trying lots of things that didn't work, and continually iterating until it got to something that worked.

Coca-Cola is now seeing bumper crops of fruit. The breakthrough part of this project—the startup idea—is that if it can do this with mangoes in India, the company figured it could likely do the same in other countries with other crops. It knew it needed to find a way to scale these results to meet its 2020 goal of tripling the juice business globally.

In 2010, Coca-Cola launched Project Nurture, a partnership with the NGO TechnoServe and the Bill & Melinda Gates Foundation, to teach these same skills to farmers in Uganda and Kenya. This time the company added passion fruit cultivation to the curriculum.

That year, Coca-Cola trained an estimated forty thousand farmers, of which nearly seventeen thousand were women. Those farmers produced eighteen thousand tons of fruit. The company is hoping that eventually at least 30 percent of the farmers it trains will be women, and that this technique will help participating farmers double their income.

As a bonus, the company launched Minute Maid Mango Nectar in Kenya, the first product to use juice sourced from Project Nurture.

After learning about quality specifications, logistics, and price negotiations from the NGO, the farmers have formed co-ops and are now shipping mangoes and passion fruit to the Middle East.

It's a win-win when a company can align a region's socioeconomic interests with its own business interests. They learn and thrive; the company learns and grows.

The key is to understand that you won't get it right the first time—the only way to maintain the kind of agility you need is to focus on learning by doing.

Minimum Viable Product

There's a lot we can all learn from how startups develop products. When companies like Twitter, Foursquare, or Evernote were startups, they first began designing features or products by learning what end users really wanted or needed, which was often very different from what the developers thought they wanted. The only way to do this is to get a very rough version to market—in front of actual users—as quickly as possible. The process for doing this is often called hack, release, repeat.

The goal is to design a *minimum viable product*, a product that's just good enough to get in front of users—real people, often early adopters—who can use the product and give feedback on what's working and what isn't, as quickly as possible. Then developers go back and hack, or tear their product apart, to make it better, stronger, or more intuitive to the user. The more users like it, the more users. The more users, the faster the startup can get to scale.

A minimum viable product is a type of prototype. It's the just-good-enough version of a product.

This process is second nature for the startup community, but you don't have to be a startup to work this way. Some big companies, like Apple, are great at this. Every time Apple releases a new iPhone, iPad, or operating system upgrade, they know the release is not perfect—it's just the next release. In Apple's case, early adopters start queuing up for days in advance just to be among the first to get the newest release, despite knowing that subsequent versions will be better.

Now, no one would pay hundreds of dollars for a minimum viable product. So, when Apple finally launches a new product, it's no longer minimum; it's closer to viable. The point is that they know they are going to change something later—they simply draw the line on how perfect the new release has to be. This approach allows Apple to move quickly, getting its products to market faster than if they were trying to design fully integrated, timeless classics, designed never to stray too far from their original design.

Any company can use this approach to design. Let's look at how we used this approach to redesign a core element that is fundamental to the company's food-service business, a multibillion-dollar business in North America.

Coke Case: Freestyle Fountain Machine

Anyone who has ever stepped up to a fountain machine at McDonald's in New York City or Burger King in London and fills her cup with Coke is getting her beverage in the way in which it was originally designed to be delivered one hundred years ago.

As we saw in chapter 2, the first Coca-Cola ever sold was dispensed not in the green iconic bottle that would eventually become its signature package, but at a soda fountain in Jacobs' Pharmacy in Atlanta.

While the mechanism for delivering fountain drinks—pour syrup in glass, add ice and carbonated water, stir—evolved, it was at a glacial pace. It wasn't until the Great Depression that fountain technology moved beyond the fancy porcelain syrup urns that Asa Candler, the company's first marketing guru, had dispensed to his best customers.

Innovation was hampered by factors beyond The Coca-Cola Company's control. Only a few companies controlled the manufacture of fountain machines, and their interest was in designing machines that had the most appeal to the widest audience—standardization across the industry.

By 1998, the fountain business accounted for nearly 22 percent of the 9.6 billion cases of soda sold in the United States. In 2005, the company was responsible for about 75 percent of sales in that channel.

As Coca-Cola's portfolio of brands grew, its fountain machines couldn't adapt. The way in which they were designed didn't enable the flexibility or sustainability it needed to drive growth.

A typical machine in a restaurant or cafeteria could only dispense between six and eight different choices. So, while people were becoming increasingly enthusiastic about things like Coke Zero and Cherry Coke, they were typically limited to just a few choices: Coke and Diet Coke, Barq's Root Beer, Minute Maid Lemonade, and a few others. If they wanted to shift from Coca-Cola to caffeine-free beverages in the late afternoon, there weren't many options. And, if they wanted a noncarbonated beverage, they were pretty much out of luck. It's been this way for at least the last fifty years.

In addition, as the business grew, the company wanted to investigate ways to save on transportation costs. It knew that if it could increase the concentration of the beverage base, it could have an alternative to the big, five-gallon bag-in-a-box containers that it had traditionally used. Less weight meant reduced costs, and a smaller carbon footprint. However, getting that highly concentrated liquid through the valves was a technological hurdle.

The company knew it needed to design a modular system.

It needed a solution that could scale internationally, but was flex-ible enough to adapt to the particular circumstances of its location and desires of consumers, and also be easy for Coca-Cola's customers—the restaurateurs and food service operators—to manage.

Developers explored many different kinds of technologies—far beyond the beverage industry. For example, from the pharmaceutical industry they learned about a microdosing technology that allowed highly concentrated flavors to be dispensed via cartridges instead of traditional, bulky bags in boxes. It also allowed the company to in-crease the number of flavors it could offer exponentially.

After many prototypes, a multidisciplinary team launched ver-sion 1.0 of a fountain machine called Freestyle. With v1.0 it really focused on choice. The team realized that, as the company added new choices, it was actually creating new occasions for people. So, for example, in a typical restaurant, caffeine-free Diet Coke would not be in the top eight or ten choices. It would never have made sense to put it in a Top 10 machine. But, they discovered, after three in the afternoon, it's in the top three. And, as people became more calorie conscious, consumption of low and no-calorie beverages was likely to increase. The company needed to be able to expand those choices as that market grew. Ultimately, developers decided to in-clude seventy low-calorie options, and some thirty others, for a total of more than one hundred different choices.

Transporting those forty-pound bags of beverage base also be-came a thing of the past. Instead, flavors arrive in cartridges via freight carriers or food-service distributors, cutting 30 percent of the solid waste and volume out of the supply chain, just by elimi-nating the need to transport water. The cartridges themselves were designed to feel both robust and familiar, so that crew members at restaurants—often young, relatively unskilled workers—could feel confident switching them in and out, much as they would an ink car-tridge in a printer.

*Connecting Freestyle to the Web allows the company
to create much more speed to market with new
products, but also helps it learn much faster about
what its customers really need.*

Since each restaurant's consumption pattern is unique, there's no standard order. An average case has about eleven different cartridges, and it's always a different mix. To figure out how to customize such a delivery, researchers studied how companies like Pottery Barn and Williams Sonoma picked their orders.

Similarly, the machines can create error logs, telling Coca-Cola technicians when things aren't working the way they that should. "The machines call home every night," says Jennifer Mann, vice president and general manager, Coca-Cola Freestyle. "We can track their service history, and push through software fixes, before the customer ever experiences them. That's a huge advantage. Since Coca-Cola products have some of the highest profit margins of any of the products in a restaurant, it's very important for the restaurant operator to have everything functioning well at all times."

To capture enthusiasm for the mix-your-own-drink phenomenon, the company also launched a Facebook page dedicated to Freestyle, which lets consumers share the drink recipes they concocted. A Freestyle app allows fans to save their custom combinations and then scan the app at a machine and have it mix up their creation. The response was overwhelming, as exotic recipes poured in. Each fan can post his special drink recipe on his Facebook page along with his picture.

One of the unexpected results of the company's new ability to capture consumption data—everything from usage patterns in different geographies to wacky flavors that teens are creating and sharing with each other through social media—is that Coca-Cola now has an extraordinary window into what people are really drinking. That information has already begun to translate into decisions on new products in its retail business, surfacing trends earlier, and enhancing its speed to market.

As it turned out, the best research the team did was just watching people waiting in line and using the machine.

"We're learning to address multiple needs, find commonalities, and, with an iterative process, develop multiple solutions at the same time. And we're doing it two to three times faster than we did with our original project management approach," says Mann.

Business results have been more robust than Coca-Cola ever anticipated. Some two-thirds of consumers who know about Freestyle say they actually choose where they go to eat or to a movie based on whether the venue has a machine. The company is seeing a 30 percent increase in its sales. And the restaurants themselves are sharing in the success, with a 4 to 5 percent rise in overall traffic, and double digit increases in beverage servings.

LESSON LEARNED #10

Pull, Not Push

Okay, where do you start? In a large organization, starting anything can be daunting. In my experience, it's not really all that important where or how you start; the point is just to begin. When I first joined the company, if anyone asked to meet with me or invited me to talk about design—or almost anything—I'd go.

Starting is more about building relationships, about other people getting to know you. If you're the one leading the change, the goal is to start learning as quickly as possible, by learning the stuff they don't put in manuals or post on the Intranet. If it's your responsibility to get your organization focused on design, jump in.

The most strategic thing would be to focus on your most valuable market or brands but, for me, it's never that logical; it's more relational. I call this *going where the action is*: focusing on the markets, teams or people who are pulling you into their problems. It's much easier to work with people who want you in their world than to try to push your ideas on people who may not be receptive.

One of my earliest opportunities arose when the Indonesian business unit president called and asked me to come speak to his leadership team about design and design thinking. When I got there, we walked the streets and experienced what was going on. We even sent one of our designers to Jakarta for a three-month assignment just to be on the ground, ready to help. We tried a bunch of things—many that didn't work. It was clunky, hard, and frustrating but there was strong support and we learned a lot.

Once you've begun, the next step becomes more critical. At that point, you need to be very sensitive to momentum—you have to start being able to see patterns emerging. You will begin to get a sense of what will stick and what won't, what you should focus on, and what you need to do to get some quick wins. Momentum breeds momentum.

In my case, the Indonesian job opened the doors to an opportunity to build our strength in design and design thinking across Latin America. It was a dream come true for me, but that would have never happened if we hadn't gone to Jakarta first. By the time we got to Latin America, we were able to move much faster, think more holistically, and scale our efforts much better than we did in Indonesia.

Key Takeaway: Pull is always better than push—go where your help is most needed and wanted first. A few quick wins will help you build momentum for other challenges.

Then, Do it Faster

In short: Speed is the critical differentiator in a world driven by relentless change and daunting unpredictability. Every company wants to be able to get its products out faster and better than its competitors. Here's the rub: Can you be both faster and better at the same time? Doesn't speed often lead to products that are badly designed, or disappointing to a brand's best customers?

The key to success is learning by doing. Constant iteration, a willingness to test ideas with real customers and gauge their responses, then pivot if they're not working, is critical. Rather than betting the ranch on a big idea, small tests can help a team determine if an idea has the legs for a bigger rollout.

Startups move fast—they have to. Every day is potentially life or death. Big companies look at this kind of speed with amazement: "How can they move that fast, and why can't we?" But what's not easy to see is that startups are actually designed to move that fast—they are built for speed.

Everything from their org chart to their partnerships to their products, are designed to create maximum flexibility, giving them the ability to pivot when necessary.

Every company can be this nimble if it designs for it. Using design to learn by doing—using minimum viable products to learn as fast as possible—actually reduces risk and the fear of failure for everyone. You don't have to be a startup to move as fast as a startup, but it never happens by chance—only by design.

CHAPTER 6

Leaner

"The future belongs to the discontented."

Robert Woodruff, president, The Coca-Cola Company,
1923–1954

When I was in eighth grade, I had a school assignment to write a paper every week. Every Saturday morning, one of my parents would drive me to our local library. I'd take out my index cards, notebook, and pen and get started. Thinking back, I can't remember a single subject, or any of the papers I wrote, but I can remember exactly how I began my research on the various topics—opening the *World Book Encyclopedia*.

After a few weeks, I actually began to enjoy the process. All those Saturdays in the library must be one reason why I'm a superfan of Wikipedia. I'm on the site at least once a day. It's so easy to use. There's another reason to love it even more. It's open to everyone, and wouldn't exist without people sharing what they know. Wikipedia is a collaboratively edited encyclopedia with over 23 million articles, and one hundred thousand editors in over 285 languages, written by thousands of people who constantly update, edit, and change the entries.

The days of driving to a library and using a printed encyclopedia to research a topic seem so archaic. In fact, the whole system now seems kind of quaint.

World Book used to publish a new set of encyclopedias each year. If you wanted to stay current, you had to buy the yearly update. World Book was very centralized and rule based. If you wanted to know something about penguins in Patagonia and they didn't think it was important—sorry—no penguins. They made the rules, not you.

Wikipedia is designed for agility.

With Wikipedia, entries are updated as news happens. New stuff gets added daily. However, unlike World Book, Wikipedia is decentralized and self-organized, with content written by 45 million registered users and many others who are anonymous. All of the content is modular. Like Legos, Wikipedia has fixed and flexible elements. Its Web site's format is fixed but its content is quite flexible. This allows everyone at Wikipedia to learn fast and adapt to what users really want.

World Book is designed to be a Lamborghini—a beautiful integrated system—a classic. Wikipedia is designed like a big box of Legos—a modular system.

Before we dive into our last chapter, let's do a quick review.

Scale and Agility

In chapter 1, we established that design is about intentionally connecting things to solve problems. Then we introduced Simon Sinek's

Golden Circle framework to help us understand the relationship between the *Why,* the *How,* and the *What* of design.

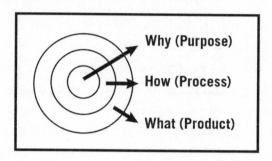

In chapter 2, we went into depth on how to design for *scale.* In this case, our purpose or *Why* was scale. Our process or *How* was to simplify, standardize, and integrate. And our product example, our *What,* was a Lamborghini.

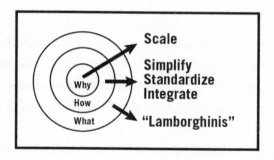

In chapter 3, we focused on complexity, and why every company needs not only scale but also agility to adapt to a world that's changing faster than ever.

In part 2, we introduced a different approach to design we called *Designing for Agility.* In this approach, we're looking at how startups use design to be smarter, faster and leaner. Our purpose, or *Why,* is agility. Our process, or *How,* is to Learn, Build, Measure. And our product example, our *What,* is Legos.

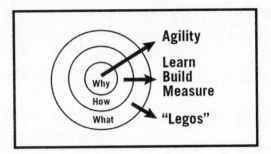

In this chapter we're going to focus on how design can actually make a company leaner: how you can design to use fewer people, less time, and less money to get better results.

We're going to focus on how modular systems enable much more openness and collaboration, which is critical for agility.

Open, Not Closed

We've defined a *system* as a set of elements and behaviors that connect to do one thing. We've discussed how integrated systems, like Lamborghinis, create scale and modular systems, like Legos, create agility. We've also shown how modular systems are designed differently from integrated systems.

In chapter 5, we noted that there are two things that make a product or service modular:

1. *Modular systems have fixed and flexible elements.*
2. *All the elements connect in the same way.*

But there is a third aspect we haven't yet discussed.

3. *Modular systems are designed to be open.*

This openness makes it easier for everyone to take part in the design process, to contribute new ideas, elements, and behaviors into the system.

Open systems allow others to play in your sandbox.

Why is that important? Modular systems enable more collaboration and create much more diversity. Opening up and letting others in allows the system to develop in ways it never could by remaining closed. Crowd-sourcing, crowd-funding, coworking, and open-source development are all based on this kind of approach to design.

To be clear, just because a system is modular, doesn't mean it's open. If we go back to our Legos example, we can see that while Legos is a great example of a modular system, it's not an open, but a *closed* modular system.

You may be a superfan, own every Lego set ever made, and have some really great ideas for new products, but you'll never get them into next year's new release from Lego. You could even design and make new bricks with your 3D printer, then send them to Lego's headquarters in Billund, but it won't make a difference. Legos is a *closed* system.

While it may seem counterintuitive, opening up,
sharing, and allowing others to codesign, develop,
and build your products actually makes you leaner.

When a company opens up, it can tap into the creativity, resources, and passion outside its own team, group, function, or company, often for free. Most people love to share; they just don't know how. Most of the time, it's not easy.

In chapter 5 we said that one of the critical aspects of designing modular systems is that there must be a few things that are fixed, such as the way that Legos connect. This is especially true for open systems.

On Wikipedia, you can't change the fonts, write your entry in iambic pentameter, or add funny YouTube videos of cats. There are rules that everyone must follow. With open systems, such rules or fixed elements must be simple enough so that everyone can participate. Open systems depend on others being able to add to the system easily. On Wikipedia, for example, physicists are invited to write about thermodynamics. Poets are encouraged to improve the entry on Robert Pinsky. This is what enables others to flock, swarm, and join together. Once you have that, you can do things you could never do alone. It's this openness that creates the agility. The key is knowing when and how to design each kind of system to get the results that you need as a company.

> *When you're designing an open system, the goal is to enable sharing.*

No one person is expert in all the fields that Wikipedia covers. It wouldn't work unless everyone got on board.

This way of designing can actually be a lot of fun. Remember, you're not designing one perfect system, releasing it, and scaling it. You're constantly in design mode with lots of people. This allows you to try things very quickly, and to collaborate with many others. Everybody feels as though he or she owns the system.

Compare that to integrated systems, where you've proven your assumptions, built a repeatable model, iterated, and optimized your product to be as perfect as possible. Then you can scale like crazy.

Despite their undeniable appeal, however, there is a downside to open systems. They are far more complex than integrated systems. For them to work, you have to motivate people to *want to* contribute. If nobody adds anything, an open system won't survive. And because it's open to everyone, things are always a little messy. That means there's an opportunity for plenty of bugs and the constant potential for things to go wrong.

However, with an open system, if you can get your whole company to join in, the very act of participation creates a lot of buzz and excitement, since everybody feels as though he or she is contributing to the company's success.

Let's look at an example of an open system we created at Coca-Cola called Design Machine.

Coke Case: Design Machine

A few years ago, I went to Jakarta, Indonesia, one of Coca-Cola's biggest growth markets. Indonesia is predicted to be the tenth-largest economy in the world by the end of the decade, and could be the sixth-largest economy by 2030.

The country is young and connected. It has one of the largest populations of teenagers in the world, and they've embraced social media and the mobile Internet with unbridled enthusiasm. They're the second biggest global population on Facebook, and Jakarta is the largest Twitter city in the world. That makes the region a critical one for us.

Shortly before I visited, we had launched Coca-Cola's first global campaign in years. The whole company was on a roll, with lots of momentum and excitement. I was expecting to see something similar to what I had just witnessed in Turkey, Mexico, and other markets—new advertising, packaging, retail displays, and signage, well executed, and integrated using our new visual identity system for Coke. I was in for a surprise.

There I stood, on a hot, humid morning, outside a convenience store, the Indonesian equivalent of a 7-Eleven, with one of our local bottlers. We were looking up at a Coca-Cola sign that was illegible from more than ten feet away. And I had to confess that I was the guy responsible for the design of the sign.

What went wrong?

Visual identity systems are really important for Coca-Cola. The company uses them to help integrate all of the ways people experience its brands, from films to packaging to retail experiences. They're designed as modular systems, providing the elements and guidance needed for all of its markets to execute. This system gives the company the kind of global consistency and local flexibility it needs.

In this case, we had created the visual identity system for "The Coke Side of Life," a new global marketing campaign, and we thought it was brilliant. Our goal was to bring new relevance to Coca-Cola.

The creative brief was based on a world of many choices, where people are "free to create their own positive reality, to be spontaneous, to listen to their hearts and to live in full color." We were on it!

We were so enthusiastic about the concept that we decided to go a little crazy. We created lots of new branding elements—flowers, musical notes, birds, flags, fish, butterflies—exploding out of a Coke bottle. The possibilities were endless. We felt as though we needed to be very creative with the brand's identity. We also took a few risks. For example, we rolled out a very colorful palette to complement Coca-Cola's signature red. And we decided to crop the Spencerian script to create a little surprise.

We launched the new visual identity system with our global advertising campaign. It was a new day—the brand was going to get a fresh new start. We were all superexcited. It was a big mistake.

Initial returns were great: The new campaign drove higher sales globally and increased market share, but implementing the campaign with the new identity system cost our company and bottlers around the world a lot of money to execute. Everyone used the new visual identity system across all of their assets: coolers, signage, cups, the umbrellas that shade tables in every city in the world, and fleets of delivery trucks. Across the globe, there are millions of these assets, and revising them is a huge capital expense.

One of the main problems was that while our branding system looked great on paper, it was very easy to get wrong. When it was done badly, it resulted in the sign I saw in Jakarta. And, since a system like this should have a minimum shelf-life of five years, but realistically be able to hold up for a decade, we were stuck with the results for a long, long time.

The "Coke Side of Life" campaign was the first global effort we had embarked on in decades. The company's prior strategy had been to turn branding decisions over to local markets completely. It was an idea that had grown out of the previous decade's globalization debate, as international brands like Coca-Cola's had tried to balance maintaining a strong, unified identity with the need for a more decentralized strategy. During that period, if bottlers in the Baltics, for example, wanted to festoon their cans with bubbles and homegrown typography, they were encouraged to let it rip.

By the end of 2005, the brand identity was a mess. We didn't have one identity for Coca-Cola; we had many different identities, all overlapping. Even in developed countries like the United States, it was chaotic.

The "Coke Side of Life" campaign debuted against that background. The branding system we had created was certainly purposeful: It did the job that we had hoped for in driving revenues and creating awareness of the brand, but it just couldn't scale or adapt the way we needed it to.

Our problem was that while we had cleverly executed an integrated campaign, I didn't truly understand the scope and scale of Coca-Cola's business. While it was true we needed to expand the meaning of Coke and create more relevance, we should have taken a different approach with the visual identity system. Instead of launching a new system to overlap onto all of the others that were already out there, we should have been much more focused on our fixed elements and much more open with our flexible elements.

We had designed a closed system; we needed an open one.

We needed an identity system that was flexible enough to be executed through point-of-sale signage in small mom-and-pop shops in China, as well as in Super Bowl films with huge audiences in the United States. It needed to be able to be localized from Jakarta to Johannesburg while continuing to build equity with fixed things like the Spencerian script, Coca-Cola Red, and advertising slogans.

In the wake of that experience, and others like it, we redesigned the visual identity system yet again.

Todd Brooks, the lead designer on the project at the time, headed to the archives for inspiration. We had one hundred years of history to stand on, and we knew that we needed to create something that people could build on for the next one hundred. "I felt the answer to the future could be found in the past," Brooks says. "I needed to understand what we had done then that we weren't doing today."

Combing through the shelves with archivist Phil Mooney and his team, Brooks came upon inspiration from a surprising source: a can from the 1970s. It was bold, it was simple; you could tell it was Coke from a distance, which was an increasingly important standard, given my unhappy recent experience.

Brooks set out to pare our flagship brand down to its core assets: the color red, the script, the ribbon, and the contour bottle. In search of an identity system that could be replicated across the Coca-Cola universe, we established a core principle that summarized the idea of an open, modular system: We kept the concept "utterly familiar yet continually surprising," but laid down some rules around it.

We reached out to U.K.–based firm Attik with a brief for a new global brand-identity system that was simple. "It was about bringing a simplicity to the language, about the bold use of the iconic bottle, a flat red, and a flat script . . . Core brands need a timeless quality," says James Sommerville, who founded the agency and is now Coca-Cola's vice president of global design.

To ensure that these new identity standards were understood throughout the hundreds of countries in which we operate, Attik and Brooks developed the fixed elements of the system, specifying in ex-cruciating detail, everything from the placement of the white ribbon that swirls down the can, to the kinds of clothes that models can wear in photographs featuring the product.

Then, we opened the system up to other teams and allowed it to emerge. The United States jumped in first. San Francisco's Turner Duckworth quickly expanded the system to add relevance for our big-gest market. Other countries soon followed the United States. The revised visual identity system for Coke worked beautifully. It created the integration and flexibility we needed internally. It was also recog-nized externally, winning the first-ever Design Grand Prix in Cannes in 2008.

We learned our lesson. With the success of Coca-Cola's rebrand-ing, we used the same approach to redesign the identities for all of our biggest brands. Once we had established our identity systems, the question was how we could get everyone to contribute to them. How could we make it easy for others to keep adding to the systems?

We needed a better way of enabling more sharing.

The answer was Design Machine, a Web-based customization tool that makes it easy to create, share, and contribute.

Design Machine enables anyone to create brand communications that are not only aligned with our global marketing strategies but also fully localized for their region.

"We came up with a standardized template for packaging," says Brooks, "that really puts rules around what our core assets are." It mandates things like where to put the Spencerian script, how to place the ribbon, and the precise shade of red, but the system also allows for remarkable flexibility.

Design Machine also creates huge cost savings.

It streamlines the process for local approval and legal review, and can reduce the usual agency/company development process from weeks to minutes. To date, Design Machine has generated over $100 million in cost savings with more than thirty-five thousand users in over two hundred countries.

Design Machine also gives us sharper focus. We measure everything, but really drill down on the metrics that drive effectiveness and efficiency. We can track who uses what content—what's working and not working—and remove the elements that are less effective.

"We needed to develop a collaborative platform that could drive capability around the world," says Gerardo Garcia, global group design director. "A modular design that would allow us to scale was critical."

The tool manages two seemingly contradictory things simultaneously: It builds brand equity through fixed standards, and enables rampant creativity from the farthest reaches of the company through a modular open system.

"If you can move wisdom, learning, and knowledge to the fringes of your company faster than your competitor, you can get an advantage," says Joe Tripodi, who was Coca-Cola's chief marketing officer at the time.

There's a huge edge if you can break down barriers to communication and information sharing, which is a challenge in small shops as well as giant corporations. "I want people to poke their heads out of silos and say, 'Hey, I've got this design challenge here in Brunei, but I don't need to solve it myself,'" Tripodi says. "Give them tools to find the solution instead of reinventing the wheel."

Design Machine gives us a platform for open development and user-generated content. We learn constantly, measure what matters, and pivot when we need to, so that we can move as fast as possible.

LESSON LEARNED #11

Make it Easier to Do the Right Thing

Peter Drucker once said, "Management is doing things right; leadership is doing the right things."

When it comes to design, how can you make it easier for your team, your organization, or your company, to do both? How can you make it easier to manage how you design, and even take a leadership position through design?

It all comes down to creating the right tools. Most people want to do the right thing but, especially in large organizations, it can actually be easier to do the wrong thing. Your job is to change that, to make it easier to do the right thing and harder to do the wrong thing.

For example, most companies have two very common needs that affect how they use design.

First of all, if they make fast moving consumer goods (CPG industry) like we do, they need a way to keep track of all of the elements that go into designing stuff: the ingredients of their products, the different packages, the branding elements, and the communications. The second need is less visible. I call it *the need to create*. Most people, especially in large companies, want to leave their fingerprints on the brands that they work with. And that's natural, right?

When you take a job that is connected to a big, global, iconic brand, you want to be able to look back and say, "I did that," or "I made that." You want to know that you've had some kind of influence on making the brand a little bit better or more successful than before you came to it.

To build a design-driven culture, you need to be able to manage all your assets very efficiently but also enable everyone to use those assets very effectively.

In most large organizations, different processes, standards, and rules often don't connect to each other, so people find shortcuts to try to get things done. In some cases, ineffective systems can actually create confusion, increase costs, and slow things down by making doing the wrong thing easier.

Using an agile approach to design—leveraging modular open systems—can help make it easier for almost anyone inside any function in your company to do the right thing.

For instance, if you want everyone to design better PowerPoint presentations, design a system—a template with easy-to-use guidelines.

If you want your team to have more effective meetings, design a system: name the types of meetings, set limits on times for each type, clarify the roles and responsibilities, and create a knowledge sharing platform so the learning can be shared.

If you want to create more openness across your team, design a system. Schedule a lunch hour and invite two or three people to tell a story about a time that they failed at something. Ask them first to tell the story, then illustrate three things that they learned from it.

At Coca-Cola we've done these things and a lot more. The point is that you can make it easy to do the right thing by design.

Key Takeaway: Designing the right tools makes it easier to do the right thing.

Emergence

Birds flock together to navigate south for the winter. Ants swarm together in the Amazon and devour a whole field in minutes. Unemployment, debt, and consumer fears connect in people's brains and an economy goes into recession. A rival posts a compromising video of a politician on YouTube and the man's (or woman's) career is over before he can finish his morning coffee.

All of these are examples of what's called *emergence*. Emergence is a wonky word usually reserved for scientists, economists, and systems theory geeks like me. Emergence is when individual elements interact or work together to create something new, something that couldn't be created if each element acted alone. The word may be unfamiliar, but we've all seen emergence in action.

Let's start with a basic understanding of emergence to better understand how we can design for it.

For example, economists study how the rate of investment, population growth, technological change, and other factors work together to create emerging economies. Countries like China, Brazil, Russia, India, Mexico, Indonesia, and Turkey are the best examples. These countries are considered to be in a transitional phase, in that they are emerging from being developing to being developed markets. Each macroeconomic element connects with the others to create growth. No one factor alone is sufficient.

For a less serious example, look at Minecraft. Minecraft has no marketing budget, but the game has sold over 12 million copies on Xbox 360, 15 million copies on PC, and nearly 54 million copies across all platforms with more than 100 million registered users. Why? Minecraft has no specific goals for the player to accomplish, allowing players an almost unlimited amount of freedom in choosing how to play the game. It also has a wide variety of user-generated content such as modifications of the Minecraft code, called mods, enabling an almost endless variety of gameplay changes. Each of these elements works with the others to allow the game to develop and grow.

In the startup community, a good example of emergence is Kickstarter. In November 2010, Scott Wilson, a Chicago designer, posted his idea—a watch that grafted an iPod Nano onto an aluminum case—on the popular funding platform for creative projects. The idea had been rejected by a variety of companies, but Wilson believed in it enough to give it one more try. Within a week, he had raised $400,000 from five thousand backers. Within a month, he had amassed a war chest of $1 million from 13,500 people in fifty countries. Kickstarter had enabled Wilson's project to emerge.

But how does this work? What makes ants, birds, economies, video game players, and Kickstarter investors act this way?

Emergence relies on self-organization. To create emergence, you have to design in a way that creates order between diverse elements so lots of people can share lots of stuff.

The order must be spontaneous and decentralized, not directed or controlled by anyone. It must come from within the system and feel intuitive to everyone involved.

Here's another example. I love shopping on Zappos.com. It's easy to search, easy to shop, easy to buy, and easy to return anything that I don't like. The whole process feels very seamless and in my control. I'm sure a million other people would agree. That's no accident. Zappos is designed so that people come first. The user experience is preeminent. One of the best things about Zappos is that each product is rated by actual users. So, for example, if I see a pair of boots that I like, I carefully check the reviews, written by real people, not Zappos' marketing staff, before I order. They'll tell me if the sizing runs large or small, if the boots are comfortable from the get-go, or need to be broken in, or if they provide enough arch support. They use video and easy-to-understand language. If the boots don't work—no problem. They've designed a three-step return process that makes sending things back a no-hassle experience.

Zappos is designed to be very social. When I shop on Zappos, I join the swarm, invariably doing what they hope I will do: buy more shoes. If I find a pair I especially like, I will create content by posting a review or sharing with my friends. This is, of course, good for them but also good for me.

Zappos is also designed to enable emergence. By 2008, its culture and customer service had become such a legend in the eyes of other companies that it launched Zappos Insights, a $39.95 per month subscription video service that lets companies ask questions about the Zappos way, and get answers from actual Zappos employees.

Let's look at another Coke Case. This time we'll show how designing for emergence can go beyond product development into training and support services.

Coke Case: 5by20 Program

In chapter 5, we saw how an investment in tiny businesses that are inaccessible by normal delivery systems is paying off, both for Coca-Cola and for the 2500 individual entrepreneurs who run them. The manual distribution centers (MDCs) in Africa are also a great example of modular systems that are designed to change over time.

A substantial number of the MDCs' owners and managers are women, many of whom make as much as $20,000 to $30,000 per year, depending on their area and the time of year. In regions where people often live on one dollar per day, their success lifts whole families out of poverty. In addition to creating jobs in the distribution center, the MDCs have been shown to generate enough income to support an estimated 41,000 dependents.

The success of that program got Coca-Cola thinking about the role of women in economic empowerment. Data show that investing in women is a good strategy. In the Philippines, women own or operate more than 86 percent of small neighborhood stores that sell our products. In developing countries, half of all farmers are women. All in all, women make up a significantly high percentage of the key segment of our value chain.

MIT economist Esther Duffo found that when women earn money, they're more likely than men to spend it on food, while men tend to spend it on alcohol and tobacco. Additionally, women generally reinvest 90 percent of their income in their families, in the health and education of their children, versus the 30 to 40 percent that men invest.

Women are not only pillars of our business but pillars of their communities.

Coca-Cola realized that if it could empower more women, it could boost a region's economy, increasing its buying power. Good for them, good for the company.

So, in 2010, the company launched an initiative that it called *5by20*. Its goal was to enable 5 million women in one hundred countries to earn a sustainable income by 2020. This is not about just writing a check. The idea is to train women to become entrepreneurs and self-supporting, which will have a much more lasting impact.

"Unless you have a sustainable community, you can't have a business," says Charlotte Oades, Coca-Cola's global director for women's economic empowerment.

5by20 was designed to be social: it's made it easy for entrepreneurs to start their own businesses. The company didn't dictate how to do this in exact terms—it made some things fixed, and many things very flexible—but it's open to fresh ideas and exploration. 5by20 was designed to emerge. As women discovered the program, they could adapt it to their own circumstances. In some countries, women would use the education and financing to start distribution programs; in others, they would use it to fund little shops. It could work across geographies, cultures, and languages, gaining traction as it gained scale.

This open system also allows the company to quickly adopt new partners in its journey. Coca-Cola has partnered with the International Finance Corporation (IFC), UN Women, and others around the world.

By designing its 5by20 program to be modular and open, the company has the flexibility it needs to adapt to local conditions around the world.

Preeti Gupta is one of the women in this program. She lives about fifteen kilometers from Agra in India, in a little town with very little electricity. Weeks can go by without any power.

Once Preeti married, she was expected to stay home and raise her family. However, she was eager for her children to have a better life, so she opened a little shop in her living room, selling drinks, snacks, and grain.

It wasn't easy. She and her husband borrowed from relatives and mortgaged their personal belongings to start the shop.

In 2010, Coca-Cola helped out by installing a solar panel on her roof. It let her power a small cooler and sell cold drinks, a luxury in her community. The solar panel had other benefits as well. It meant she could keep the store open longer hours. Her kids could study at night. And her shop became a community magnet.

"The solar cooler has helped me a lot," she says. "Customers come here to charge their mobiles and charge their lanterns in daylight so they can use them in nighttime. Also customers come to our shop when they see the lights and others are out of electricity."

It doesn't hurt that those customers are likely to kick back with a frosty beverage as they wait for their mobile phones to charge.

Preeti's income has escalated, and she now has high hopes of sending her children to a good school. Plus, she says, she's gained the respect of her family.

The program takes different forms in different countries. In Brazil, 5by20 sponsors financial workshops. In India, an air-conditioned bus, the Parivartan, becomes a traveling classroom, bringing education to the women so that they don't have to travel. In Nairobi, The Coca-Cola Company and its bottling partners help young women raise seed capital and offer marketing support for their young businesses. That's an important boost for an age bracket, from sixteen to twenty-four, when unemployment is high.

While a program like this is very complicated, Coca-Cola has a simple and actionable metric that it uses to stay focused.

5by20, that easy-to-remember metric, has brought a huge amount of clarity and focus for the company around the world.

By the end of 2012, Coca-Cola had 5by20 programs in Brazil, China, Costa Rica, Egypt, Haiti, India, Kenya, Mexico, Nigeria, the Philippines, South Africa, and Thailand. The 5by20 program has helped more than 300,000 women become economically independent, not a bad start toward the goal of 5 million by 2020.

Focus

There is one thing that is common for both startups and big companies. To win, you have to *focus*. Without focus, it's easy to waste resources, like time, money, and people. For big companies, a lack of focus creates inefficiency and inhibits the ability to execute. This problem keeps CEOs awake at night: how can they help everyone in their company act like an owner and use the company's resources in the way in which they would use their own.

It's different for startups. Everyone *is* an owner. If the startup survives, everyone wins. If the startup fails, everyone loses. So, staying focused is a matter of life and death.

There is a great tool that startups use to stay focused on what really counts—it's called the "One Metric That Matters." As the name implies, it's the one indicator of real progress. In their book, *Lean Analytics,* Alistair Croll and Benjamin Yoskovitz say it this way:

At any given time, you'll be trying to answer a hundred different questions and juggling a million things. You need to identify the riskiest areas of your business as quickly as possible, and that's where the most important question lies. When you know what the right question is, you'll know what metric to track in order to answer that question. That's the OMTM (One Metric That Matters).

So what's *your* OMTM? What's the one thing you need to measure in your program, your project, or your team that is fundamental to success? What's the one metric that's easy for everyone to understand, and that's immediate, actionable, comparable, and fundamental to your project, your initiative, or your business?

You don't have to be in a startup to use this powerful tool. Don't be fooled by measuring things that make everyone feel good but don't really tell you if you're moving forward.

For instance, let's say you're planning a two-day workshop for your team involving a new method or process. A lot of people may sign up for the workshop and even come to the first hour or day. However, even if 150 sign up for the two-day class, if on day two you only have fifteen people in the room, maybe your invitation was better than the actual content of workshop. Your OMTM shouldn't be the number of signups, it should be the number of showups for day two.

One of the OMTMs Coca-Cola has created is around the packaging it uses in its products. In 2009, the company set a goal of sourcing 25 percent of our PET plastic for packaging from recycled and renewable materials by 2015. This easy to remember (but hard to do) metric has created great focus for employees. It's easy to understand, actionable, and fundamental to reaching the company's sustainability commitments.

Coca-Cola has recently set a new goal to use what it calls *Plant-Bottle* Packaging in 100 percent of its PET packaging by 2020. As we'll see, PlantBottle is not only the name it uses for the material but is actually another great example of a very open modular system.

Coke Case: PlantBottle Packaging

In the vast, rolling plantations of southern Brazil, sugar-cane fields stretch as far as the eye can see. The tall perennial grass, with its tough jointed stalks, is the world's largest crop.

But while most of the world thinks of cane as the source of the sugar that flavors everything from chocolate to caipirinhas, Brazilians know that it's the plant's stalks that may ultimately be the more significant crop.

The fibrous, dry matter left after the cane is processed is called *bagasse*. Far from being a waste product, bagasse is unique in that it is one of the plants that can be most efficiently converted to biofuels, like ethanol. In fact, Brazil, which is the world's largest producer of sugar cane, has become so good at processing this material, that the government has mandated that 22 percent of all gasoline used in the country be composed of bioethanol.

Because it can be grown and harvested with a lighter footprint on the environment, and since it doesn't compete with food crops, sugar cane has been named an Advanced Renewable Fuel by the U.S. Environmental Protection Agency.

Turns out, a lot more than bioethanol can be made from these left-over stalks. In 2009, The Coca-Cola Company became interested in using Brazilian bagasse as a raw material for PlantBottle, the first-ever fully recyclable PET plastic bottle made partially from plants.

PET, the plastic used in most beverage products, is polyethylene terephthalate, which is composed of two compounds: ethylene glycol and terephthalic acid. It's widely recognized as a safe plastic for beverage containers, and some 60 percent of Coca-Cola's products are packaged in PET.

The sugar-cane initiative turned out to be even more successful than the company anticipated. As the project took off, Coca-Cola set a goal: to convert all of its PET plastic bottles to PlantBottle Packaging by 2020 and to find new sources of renewable, biological materials, called *biomass feedstocks*, to serve as a basis for its packaging.

To meet its goal, the company needed more than just a new form of plastic. It needed an open, modular system.

Soon, the company realized that sugarcane was only the beginning of its journey. What if it could generate the material it needs for packaging with other waste products native to other climates and regions? Corn stover—the residue left after the grain harvest—would be a natural for the American Midwest. Rice hulls are plentiful in Asia. Wood waste—branches and bark that lumber mills generate—have shown promise as a source of ethanol in places like Maine and in Northern Europe. In the future, it may even be possible to use algae to produce the materials we need.

The challenge is to find the local feedstocks that are sustainable and don't compete with food, but are the waste byproducts of food production. They need to exist in large enough quantities that it makes sense economically to build a plant to process them, and are close enough to that facility, so that you don't lose the environmental benefits by having to truck the materials in from a long distance. Coca-Cola is partnering with the World Wildlife Fund, and eight other consumer brand companies, in the Bioplastic Feedstock Alliance to ensure that the plants we're targeting are being grown and harvested sustainably.

"The majority of our products are produced locally," says Scott Vitters, head of Coca-Cola's global PlantBottle Packaging program. "We're not shipping products all over the world. Because of that local production, we can actually shift the type of packaging we use for local markets."

For example, India is already using molasses—a byproduct of processing sugar cane, grapes, or sugar beets—to produce ethylene glycol. It's one of the two products used in PlantBottles. So, plastic Coca-Cola bottles on the Indian subcontinent, for example, don't travel far after they're produced.

Coca-Cola's ultimate goal is to figure out how to replace the other 70 percent of the PET mix, the terephthalic acid (PTA) for large-scale production. While scientists have been able to do this in the lab, producing it at scale has been a tougher nut to crack. Ultimately, the company's long-term target is to realize a 100 percent renewable, fully recyclable, plastic bottle. Working with technology partners, it has already demonstrated the potential for producing such bottles, and is now working to find a way to scale it commercially on a global scale.

_____

By 2014, Coca-Cola had distributed over 20 billion PlantBottle packages in thirty-one countries, and eliminated more than 190,000 MTs of CO_2 emissions— the equivalent of over 400,000 barrels of oil.

_____

Once PlantBottle Packaging was introduced, Coca-Cola began getting calls from other consumer product goods companies eager to work with it. Like any company with a proprietary technology, it was initially hesitant to share its intellectual property. The company, after all, was in the early stages of building this product, and its supply of the material was still limited by the number of plants capable of turning, for example, sugarcane into the material it needed.

But after the tenth or twelfth call, the company started to think about the issue in a different way. "We realized we had an innovation that we truly believe is transformational, and should be applied across the industry," says Vitters.

Coca-Cola opened up—it knows that sharing makes it leaner.

Strategically, it made more sense for the company to share this technology than to keep it just for itself. Not only would it be better for the planet if more companies could use biomass as part of their packaging instead of petroleum, but if Coca-Cola wanted to be able to move as quickly as it could, partnering with the right company could, potentially, encourage more suppliers to get on board. Of course, it would also help offset some of the risks involved in the investments it was making, as well as speed up the process.

When the company got a call from H. J. Heinz, it knew it had found the perfect partner. I like to think of Heinz as the Coca-Cola of ketchup: the gold standard for the category. The two companies historically share a lot of the same values, and their trust among consumers is very high.

Naturally, people don't buy ketchup at the same rate as, say, Coke

Zero. While in the past, Coca-Cola might have been looking to partner with a company that did a higher volume of business, in this case it realized that a ketchup bottle actually offered something a Coke bottle didn't: It had longevity. That Heinz ketchup bottle sits on a kitchen counter, or in a restaurant, for a lot longer than a beverage at lunch. It's there where people are hanging around, waiting for their burgers, beaming its little "Guess what's in this bottle?" message to anyone with the curiosity to take a look. The number of impressions those bottles have over the course of a year is incredible. Since 2011, Heinz has shipped more than 200 million ketchup bottles in PlantBottle containers.

In 2012, the company created a Plant-PET technology collaborative, including Ford Motor Company, H. J. Heinz Company, Nike, Inc., and Procter & Gamble to find a way to create 100 percent renewable polyester plastic made entirely from plants for use in everything from clothing and footwear to automotive fabric and packaging.

In 2013, at the Los Angeles Auto Show, Ford introduced a demonstration model of its popular plug-in hybrid car, the Ford Fusion Energi, outfitted with first-ever fabric covering for seat cushions and head restraints, all made with PlantBottle technology.

Happily, these partnerships have catalyzed movement in the supply chain, so that there are now many companies eager to build plants to process the biomass that PlantBottle uses.

This approach—designing PlantBottle Packaging as an open, modular system—increases the likelihood of Coca-Cola being able to deliver on the scenario we sketched out in the beginning of the chapter: bottles made from orange peels in Asia, tree bark in Russia, and corn stalks in Nebraska. It could happen sooner than we expected.

LESSON LEARNED #12

Create a Canvas

Lean startups do one thing that big, established companies sometimes struggle with. They focus on their business model from day one and constantly iterate every piece of it while they develop their idea. Said another way, they think holistically about the business while they're designing it, rather than in silos.

To be fair, this is a lot easier for startups to do, since the startup is usually just two or three cofounders in a big room, rather than a matrixed organization with multiple functions, subfunctions, and geographies.

One tool that most startups use that helps them stay lean is called a *Lean Canvas*. It's modeled on another similar tool called the *Business Model Canvas*. There are many variations of this tool out there, but the version I like best, and the one we use, is the one created by lean startup guru and advisor Ash Maurya.

PRODUCT			MARKET	
Problem: Top 3 problems	Solution: Top 3 solutions ——— Key Metrics: Key activities you measure	Unique Value Proposition: Single, clear compelling message why you are different and worth paying attention	Unfair Advantage: Can't be easily copied or bought ——— Channels: Path to customers	Customer Segments: Target customers
Cost Structure: Customer Acquisition Costs Distribution Costs Hosting People, etc.			Revenue Streams: Revenue Model Life Time Values Revenue Gross Margin	

I like how you can use one page to summarize the key assumptions or problems you need to address with regard to both the product and the market. It captures all of the critical building blocks of the business model simply, and creates an easy way to understand how the business operates.

Of course, you don't have to be a startup to use this tool. It's quite valuable no matter what stage your company is in, or what you do inside the company. By giving you a sense of the whole project at a glance, a canvas can save you a lot of time and money developing your product, or platform, or whatever you're working on.

Key Takeaway: To think holistically about what you're designing, start by creating a canvas.

Finally, Get Leaner

In short: We've seen how, when it comes to innovation, more ideas are better than one. More is more. Big companies *get* this. The hard part for most of them is actually doing it: How do you open up and incorporate new and different ideas into your supply chain, your product development, your routes to market, or your marketing programs?

The only way to do this is to actually design systems that are both modular and open. The benefit to this approach, beyond its ability to generate fresh ideas, is that open systems can make any company leaner. And lean systems not only cost less cost but also take less time—in short, more for less. When you design for agility, and let others play in your sandbox, everybody wins.

Epilogue

The Next Wave

"Anyone who is creating a new product or business under conditions of extreme uncertainty is an entrepreneur whether he or she knows it or not and whether working in a government agency, a venture-backed company, a nonprofit, or a decidedly for profit company with financial investors."

Eric Ries, *The Lean Startup*

grew up surfing. Even if the closest you've ever come to surfing is watching *The Endless Summer* or *Blue Crush* with a bag of popcorn, you probably understand that surfing is all about being in the right place at the right time. Of course, you need to know how to swim, have a board, and know a little bit about how tides work. But the real skill is being able to look out into the horizon and see the sets or patterns of waves building, then positioning yourself to make the most of them.

Surfers and entrepreneurs have a lot in common.
They're both constantly searching for the next big wave.

Being able to identify patterns and make the most of them is criti-cal when trying to start a company or keep the one you have growing.

I think the next wave of innovation and entrepreneurship is build-ing; you can see it on the horizon. However, we all have to be in the right position—as individuals, as well as companies—if we to want to catch it. As we close, let's look to a future where entrepreneurship and design are democratized and available to everyone.

Catching the Next Wave

Earlier, I mentioned my own experience with entrepreneurship, and the lessons I learned as my cofounders and I tried to grow an idea into a company back in 1997.

After leaving Process1234, I took a job at Studio Archetype, which was soon acquired by Sapient. As it turned out, Sapient was doing what I had envisioned doing at Process1234, but on a much larger scale. In 1998, my wife and I moved to New York City—the East Coast epicen-ter of the dotcom boom—where things were moving very fast.

Big, established companies wanted to quickly develop e-busi-nesses. At the time, simply adding the prefix "e" or the suffix ".com" to any established company could boost its stock price dramatically, and every company wanted in.

A whole raft of entirely new, Internet-based companies was also springing up like mushrooms after a spring rain. They are now infa-mous for growing very fast, then blowing up. Their fantasy-based busi-ness models (there was much talk in that era of monetizing eyeballs, and much spending on Aeron chairs) and an unusually forgiving mar-ket created a huge economic bubble that would burst in late 2000 and early 2001.

One of the biggest meltdowns was boo.com. Boo.com was one of the first companies to adopt a business model based entirely on ecommerce, selling big fashion brands online. They spent $135M in venture capital in eighteen months, before releasing their first product. They became the poster child for dotcom excess. I remember an email from one of boo.com's founders that went viral: "Unless we raise $20 million by midnight, boo.com is dead." Launched in the fall of 1999, it was in bankruptcy by mid-May 2000.

By 2001, the lights were starting to dim. The 2001 documentary, *Startup.com*, captured the era's crazy, skewed reality perfectly. By 2002, the dotcom/e-business era was dead.

Then, something happened. At about that time, as we mentioned earlier, Steve Blank began teaching a new approach to entrepreneurship at UC Berkeley. He and Bob Dorf captured the new approach in their first book, *The Four Steps to the Epiphany*. Rather than starting big, with huge cash investments, they advocated a new approach for startups. As we said earlier, they defined a startup as a "temporary organization *searching* for a repeatable business model."

Their approach emphasized mashing up customer development and agile product development while focusing on the business model from day one. Eric Reis went on to iterate on the approach and captured it in his book, *The Lean Startup*. This method has quickly become the blueprint for how most entrepreneurs build startups around the world.

The first wave was about moving from dotcom to startup.

Now, let's fast-forward ten years, to today. We've come a long way. Founders are no longer the geeks in the garage, behind the scenes. Mark Zuckerburg, Jack Dorsey, and Elon Musk are global celebrities. TechStars, itself once a startup based in Boulder, Colorado, has its own reality TV show. And there's more: *StartUps, Startup Junkies,*

Startupland, Dragon's Den, and *Shark Tank* all turn the notion of build-ing a business into compelling entertainment so that almost anyone can start to dream about launching his or her own company. Startups are now mainstream.

On the surface, this may seem a little superficial, but it's actually good news for everyone. It's never been easier to start a business. There are new tools available that make the process easier than ever before.

Startup Weekend, a Seattle-based nonprofit, with branches in one hundred countries, helps entrepreneurs learn how to go from an idea to a startup. If you don't know how to begin, you can learn in just fifty-four hours, for one hundred bucks, in almost any city in the world.

You don't have to go to a Startup Weekend; you can download free apps and books on everything from analytics to creating a business model canvas, to how to make a great pitch. Of course, there are thou-sands of organizations around the world to help connect you with your local startup community.

What's more, you don't have to work out of your parents' base-ment, have meetings in Starbucks, or even lease office space. There are coworking spaces from New York to Nairobi to Nepal where anyone can rent a desk and a conference room: whatever you need to get your business started.

Nor do you need a rich uncle or a venture capitalist to fund your business. Many large corporations and universities have incubators or accelerator programs to help you find the funding and mentoring you need. Or you can pitch your idea on a crowd-funding site, like Kick-starter.

These new tools, communities, and access to capital have all con-tributed to today's global startup ecosystem. That's the second wave— the wave we've been riding for the last decade.

The second wave was about building a global startup ecosystem.

The ecosystem is working. In fact, it's estimated that over five hundred thousand new businesses are started every month in the United States alone—that's over 11 million people starting something on the side or quitting their day job to start the next high-growth startup like Facebook.

This is not just about the private sector. Government and nonprofits are part of the ecosystem. New York City wants to be a startup city. Colorado wants to be a startup state, in order to create the kind of innovation ecosystem we associate with Silicon Valley but on a much bigger scale. It seems to be working. In 2013 a study indicated that, in Colorado, a new startup launches every seventy-two hours.

Is that it? Have we reached our goal? Was all of this only about launching startups? You'd think that, with all the tools and a thriving, global ecosystem, there would be a lot more Evernotes, Dropboxes and WhatsApps. The Billion-Dollar Startup Club should be exploding, but it's not; building a startup into a billion-dollar company is still a dream for most. As we noted earlier, the numbers are grim: Ninety percent of all startups still fail.

Why? There's one thing that's most to blame: *scale.*

It's easier than ever to start a business, but harder than ever to scale a business.

As we've discussed, the world is constantly becoming more complex. And this creates a lot more friction and hurdles for scale.

The ironic thing is that big, established companies know how to scale but don't know how to *start*. Why? Because starting is quite different from scaling: Agility is not the opposite of scale; it has a different purpose, and process, and it creates different results.

I was asked to give a talk to the startup community in Australia. I spoke at Fishburners, a coworking space in Sydney that was gracious enough to host the event as well as stream the talk across the country. I did a quick TED-style talk, then fielded a lot of questions. I remember clicking on a slide that contrasted starting with scaling, and the room lit up. Lots of people in the room took pictures. It was clearly a hot-button issue.

While there's been a lot of emphasis on starting lean, there has been a surprising dearth of tools and information as to how to cross the chasm between starting and scaling.

Here's the difference between the two:

- Starting is all about *agility*. When you're starting, you're developing assets (your IP, your product, your brand, your retail relationships).
- Scaling is all about *leveraging* your assets to get the most value out of them.
- Starting requires lots of *exploration and rapid iteration* to get to your business model.
- Scaling is all about *standardizing and executing your business model* so that you can take advantage of network effects.
- Starting is all about *being ready to pivot* when you need to—the whole team must be ready to rethink everything if things aren't working.
- Scaling is all about *planning*—developing a core competency in planning is critical.

- Finally, starting is all about *staying lean*: moving very fast while doing the most with the least amount of resources. All startups start with constrained resources, so this is almost intuitive. But big companies think big—they think in millions and years and functions, not in hundreds and weeks and individuals.

So, what if we could make it easier for starters to scale and scalers to start?

What if we could help founders reach scale more consistently? Imagine if we could get even 10 percent more startups to scale? Or even better, what if we could cut the 90 percent failure rate in half? What would that look like?

On the big-company side, what if we could help a lot more managers avoid a Kodak moment? Not just in the United States, but in *every* country. Think about the impact that could have on our economies.

The next wave will be all about building scale-ups.

Franck Nouyrigat, cofounder of Startup Weekend, wrote a great post on Forbes.com in 2013. He introduced the general concept of a scale-up. He defined a *scale-up* as "a business in search of its maximum scalability." He suggested that we need to put as much focus on creating scale-ups as we have in the past around creating startups. I agree.

I think we have only begun to see what can happen when startups and big companies, especially multinationals, mash up to create new types of ventures. I'm not talking about big companies funding or mentoring startups. I mean when both startups and big companies understand what each brings to the table and actually codesign, building new things that couldn't happen any other way.

What would it look like if big companies opened up their assets—their brands, relationships, and distribution channels—and partnered with founders to monetize them in new ways? This could open a whole new level of diversity and economic activity within the ecosystem. Imagine more women, more seniors, more kids, more industries, more developing countries, all benefitting from a new kind of collaboration and partnership.

Culture of Doing

This kind of thinking starts to challenge the conventional notion of what it means to be an entrepreneur. Entrepreneurship is really all about *doing*. When everyone says something can't be done, entrepreneurs figure out a way to make it happen. They create the team, they find the financing, and they do the deal.

I believe you don't actually have to start your own business to be an entrepreneur. We all start new things every day: new projects, new plans, new teams, new routines. We all want them to be successful, to scale, and to be the best they can be. So, while you may never start your own business, you can at least think and act like an entrepreneur, no matter what you do.

I think that's what people mean when they say they want to create a culture of innovation. Typically, when a company says it needs a stronger culture of innovation, it has too many checkers and not enough doers, with way more emphasis on managing than doing.

Imagine if you, your company, your organization, or your community could create a culture of doing. Now, imagine if we could create that kind of culture everywhere. What if we could empower people—

anyone, everyone—to do more? We could create more jobs, healthier economies, more opportunity, more diversity—maybe even more well-being in the world.

Design's Radical Reinvention

Remember the beginning of the book, when we first discussed the many misconceptions people have about design, what it is, who owns it, and whether its purpose is to make things look better, or to change the world?

As I think back over the past decade, I'm struck by how radically the notion of design's function is changing. It has gone from being a talent and trade owned by an elite group of specialists to a democratized skill open to anyone who chooses to employ its power.

Nothing sums up that radical role change better than an experience I had a few years ago in South Africa.

Thinking Big(ger) about Design

It's February 2011, in Cape Town, and Maarten Baas is on stage in front of more than one thousand people at Design Indaba talking about torching chairs. The young Dutch designer, one of the conference's most popular speakers, is animated as he describes how he designs the chairs in his "Smoke" series by taking furniture with classical silhouettes from such famous designers as Reitveld, Eames, and Gaudi, chars them to a crisp, then covers them with lacquer to keep them from disintegrating. Collectors around the world pay thousands of dollars for his smoked artifacts.

About twenty minutes into his presentation, Baas decides to shift gears. He says that he has been up all night trying to think of a way to talk about what's on his mind. You could hear a pin drop as the audi-ence ponders what could've caused the young superstar designer such inner turmoil. We all lean forward as he tries to unleash what's inside.

Finally, he finds his footing, and launches into a spirited attack on big companies for using design as a means for creating profit.

He believed design should be free from commercial constraints—reserved for a select few—the people who really understand design.

He lampoons everyone from Nike to Apple, and calls for more of a purist approach to design—devoid of concerns around profit and value—and passionately urges the crowd to join him in his search for a higher purpose for design.

The audience, at what is arguably the largest and most international design conference in the world, is rapt, showering Baas with enthusi-astic applause as he leaves the stage. Twitter is on fire.

I was mystified: "Is he really saying that four-thousand-dollar Smoke Chairs are 'good' and products that a lot of people like and can afford are somehow 'bad'?"

I couldn't help but think about my ride in from the airport through Khayelitsha, one of the world's largest megaslums. Most people there live on fewer than two dollars per day. They worry about finding a job, education for their kids, and food for their families. Pretty safe to say they don't spend much time thinking about expensive chairs. I sat there wondering, "Is this really what design is about?" Design, by Baas's definition, seemed so *small*.

I had preceded Baas on the program, with a talk about Coca-Cola's approach to design. I focused primarily on how we try to make it easy for everyone to be better designers no matter what their title is. It wasn't nearly as sexy as charring a chair. There was polite applause.

Right after Baas's talk, I had to race for a plane to London. At the Cape Town airport, I happened to check Twitter, to see how the conference was going. My reviews weren't good. One Tweeter called me the Martha Stewart of the conference, evidently a derogatory reference to the previous year's least-favorite speaker. One writer reported that the general consensus at lunch was one of disappointment at the rank commercialism of my presentation. Another felt compelled to come to my defense, saying that although my talk wasn't all that exciting, it didn't deserve all the hate it was generating.

I should have been seen it coming. Cool cars. Sexy shoes. Crazy architecture. Exotic chairs. That's what comes to mind when most people think about design.

And why not? That's how most of us view design, because that's how it's generally served up in popular culture. Expensive coffee-table books with beautiful photography. Reality TV shows devoted to home decorating, real estate voyeurism, or young, frustrated fashionistas. Rock-star designers who create esoteric things that win awards and inhabit museums. Malls filled with so-called designer products.

The terms design and designer have become synonymous with cool, elite, luxury, sexy, out of reach for most people, and mostly reserved for the rich.

The future will look quite different. The whole model for design is changing and becoming more open, more transparent, more accessible. I believe design will be less precious, less owned by some elite professional class. There will be more sharing, more opportunity, more jobs, more shared value for everyone. Design will go from its elitist, small "d" definition, to something bigger and more expansive.

I'm no McLuhan but I think that design will be more important than ever. I'm not talking about the *industry* of design—design agencies, design education, design publications—or a special group of people who wear black T-shirts. I'm talking more about *how* we design.

As we look to the near future, we're going to see a much more democratic design than we've seen in the past. For instance, as we move toward Web 3.0, the Internet of things, *everyone* is going to need to use systems thinking, just to make sense of the world around them. Today, it's calculated that there are roughly 10 billion connected objects: phones, televisions, cars, homes, factories, appliances, shops. By 2020, this number is expected to triple to over 30 billion things, all connected through the Internet. Can you say *complexity*? We won't be able to rely on a small set of so-called designers to help us understand the interrelationships of all these individual objects. Everyone will need these skills.

Meanwhile, as the cost of 3D printers comes down and the quality of the printing and availability goes up, many predict that the long tail of things is going to explode. Imagine your fifth grader taking a class in digital fabrication. Today, 3D printing is still in the language and domain of geeks, but soon it will go mainstream. And, just as desktop printing design tools like Photoshop moved from graphic design studios and schools to anyone with the willingness to learn a new skill, so will these new tools. That will change the game. Apple won't be the only company that will say, "Designed in California, assembled in China." Basically, any company will be able to do the same thing— move the manufacturing of its products to whatever country makes the most sense.

Speaking of China, it will continue to rise until it is the world's leading economy. Most economists believe Brazil and India will be not far behind. Just think of what the world might look like in 2020 when all these trends collide. Design will be more important than ever, but only if we begin to think about it in a much bigger sense than we have in the past.

I love this line from Chris Anderson's book, *Makers:* "We're all designers now. It's time to get good at it."

In his book, *Massive Change*, designer Bruce Mau said, "It's not about the world of design, it's about the design of the world." As the world becomes more complex, we all have the opportunity to use design to make our world—our families, our communities, our companies, our cities, our countries—better, more agile and adaptable to change, if we design on purpose.

The Deep End

'M OFTEN asked to recommend books. Marketers ask me to recommend design books. Engineers ask about brand and marketing books. Designers want business books. Entrepreneurs want books about systems. Managers at big, established companies ask about innovation and entrepreneurship. And lots of people want to learn about how to create change and be better leaders.

I've found that I learn a lot through my own research—just diving into the deep end of a subject, and reading everything I can get my hands on. I've included here a list of books from my own library that I often recommend.

Systems

Bossel, Hartmut. *Systems and Models: Complexity, Dynamics, Evolution, Sustainability.* (Books on Demand, 2007). This one is for systems geeks only. If you really want to go deep into complex systems, this will provide all the detail you could possibly want.

Mau, Bruce. *Massive Change.* (Phaidon Press, 2004). I love the first line of this book: "For most of us, design is invisible. Until it fails." This book covers significant inventions, technologies, and events from 10,000 B.C. to the present.

Meadows, Donella H. *Thinking in Systems.* (Chelsea Green Publishing Company, 2008). In my opinion, this is the best book ever written on systems thinking.

Morin, Edgar. *On Complexity.* (Hampton Press, 2008). If *Systems and Models* is for systems geeks, this one's for complexity nerds.

Senge, Peter. *The Fifth Discipline: The Art and Practice of the Learning Organization.* (Doubleday, 1990). This was the book that launched my passion for systems and systems thinking.

Design

Alexander, Christopher. *A Timeless Way of Building.* (Oxford University Press, 1979). A classic textbook used in most university design programs.

Best, Kathryn. *Design Management: Managing Design Strategy, Process and Implementation* (Fairchild Books AVA, 2006). If you're setting up a design team inside a big company, this book will save you a lot of time.

Lidwell, William, et al. *Universal Principles of Design.* (Rockport Publishers, 2010). If you only read one "design book" in your lifetime, make it this one.

McDonough, William. *Cradle to Cradle: Remaking the Way We Make Things* (North Point Press, 2010). Paper or plastic? Neither. The ideas in this book have shaped the way most people think about sustainable design.

Innovation

Christensen, Clayton M. *The Innovator's Dilemma: The Revolutionary Book That Will Change the Way You Do Business* (HarperBusiness, 2011). If you work in a big, established company, it's a must-read. Its central tenet: doing everything right is not enough.

Diamandis, Peter H. *Abundance: The Future Is Better Than You Think.* (Free Press, 2012). This is a wicked problems plus optimism mash-up.

McLuhan, Marshall. *The Medium Is the Message: An Inventory of Effects* (Gingko Press, 2005). I've read this book so many times that I've lost count. McLuhan is the guy who coined the term *the global village* (pre-Internet).

Radjou, Navi, et al. *Jugaad Innovation.* (Jossey-Bass, 2012). If your context for innovation is primarily U.S.–based, expand your lens with this one. This book takes "lean innovation" to a whole new level.

Entrepreneurship

Afuah, Allan. *Business Model Innovation: Concepts, Analysis, and Cases* (Routledge, 2014). If you're looking for a comprehensive book on business models (new and old), this is it.

Blank, Steve. *The Four Steps to the Epiphany.* (K&S Ranch, 2013). Steve Blank is the guy who kick-started the whole startup movement. Before you quit your day job, read this first.

Croll, Alistair. *Lean Analytics: Use Data to Build a Better Startup Faster.* (O'Reilly Media, 2013). An essential guide for determining the metrics that matter for your budding business.

Ries, Eric. *The Lean Startup: How Today's Entrepreneurs Use Continuous Innovation to Create Radically Successful Businesses.* (Crown Business, 2011). If you're in a big company and you're trying to figure out how to build a culture of innovation, this book has solid suggestions for how to proceed.

Brands

Aaker, David A. *Building Strong Brands.* (Free Press, 2011). If you don't know anything about brand-building, this is the best book you'll ever read. If you know a lot about brand-building, this is the best book you'll ever read.

Holt, Douglas. *How Brands Become Icons.* (Harvard Business Review Press, 2004). Every wonder what makes some brands great and others simply also-rans?

Mark, Margaret, and Carol Pearson. *The Hero and the Outlaw.* (McGraw-Hill, 2001). This book helps create a bridge between left- and right-brain-driven people when it comes to brands.

Leadership

Collins, Jim. *Good to Great: Why Some Companies Make the Leap . . . And Others Don't*. (HarperBusiness, 2011). What are the things that separate the great performers from the merely good ones? Collins crunched the data to uncover the difference.

Heath, Chip, and Dan Heath. *Switch: How to Change Things When Change Is Hard*. (Crown Business, 2010). Anything these guys write is worth reading, but this is a must-read if you've been asked to lead something really big.

Ikerd, John. *Sustainable Capitalism: A Matter of Common Sense*. (Kumarian Press, August 2005). I bought this at the bookstore inside the United Nations. Let's hope this truly is the future of capitalism.

Koch, Richard. *The 80/20 Principle: The Secret of Achieving More with Less*. (Crown Business, 1998). One of those life principles you can apply to your career or your relationships to maximize your time.

MacKenzie, Gordon. *Orbiting the Giant Hairball: A Corporate Fool's Guide to Surviving with Grace*. (Viking Adult, 1998). If you don't work in a large organization, you won't get this one. If you do, you'll read it over and over for inspiration.

Pink, Daniel. *Drive*. (Multnomah Books, 2012). If you've been asked to lead a team of millennials, you'll want to get up to speed first with this one.

Stanley, Andy. *Visioneering*. (Zondervan, 2009). You can read this in an hour. It's simple, short, and powerful.

The Designing on Purpose
Manifesto

N 2009, in its annual October design issue, *Fast Company* mentioned the white paper that I wrote shortly after joining the company. I actually named it "Building Brands, by Design," but the paper quickly became known internally as the "Designing on Purpose" manifesto. Since then, many people have asked me if I could share the document. Although it's since been added to The Coca-Cola Company archives, it's never been published outside the company, and I've never passed it along. Here is the paper in its entirety.

Building Brands, by Design

David Butler, July 14, 2004

Generally, when we talk about building our brands we put a lot of emphasis on our 30-second television ads. But what about the other seconds, minutes and hours we build our brands with through web sites, point-of-sale, vending, merchandising, packaging, etc.? We could use these opportunities to not only sell but disrupt, inspire and build love for our brands through greater focus on design. Apple does it. Nike does it. Starbucks does it. Are we any less capable? We are under-leveraging design as a strategic advantage.

What do we mean by "design"?

The term *design* is actually a term that incorporates various "design" capabilities as it relates to our business: graphic design (visual identity and print), packaging design (label and form), industrial design (vehicle, mechanical), environmental design (signage, vehicles and branded spaces), fashion design (textile and fashion), interactive design (web and digital interface design) and interior design (materials and interiors).

We are one of the world's largest design companies.

We design every day at Coca-Cola. It's the couch on *American Idol*. It's the architecture for the new World of Coke. It's the look and feel of mycoke.com. It's the t-shirt worn by the Olympic torch relay team. It's over a million vending machines in Japan alone. It's the ubiquitous Coca-Cola parasol. It's the car and uniform design of our NASCAR team. It's the nightlife activation video in *the* disco in Brussels. It's the uniform worn by our security officers in Atlanta. It's the limited edition bottle designed by fashion-designer Matthew Williamson in London. It's the hand-painted sign in Indonesia.

Design can visualize strategy.

Companies that use design as a strategic advantage create things that people *have to have*. There are stories about a problem with a recruitment strategy Coca-Cola had in Spain a few years ago. Teenagers were actually stealing our point-of-sale materials. They just *had to have* them. When was the last time we had that problem—in any market?

Design can be the differentiator.

Like many other companies, we currently spend millions of dollars on design but at times think of design as decoration, almost an after-thought. But it doesn't have to be this way. We could use design at the forefront of our strategy and truly embrace it as a strategic advantage.

Design can connect.

Design is central to our brand activation programs, licensing, sports/entertainment programs, and promotions. We could have a much broader impact if we connected all of these tools together to create powerful brand experiences. The opportunity is huge. We already make the investments. Why not make them more strategically?

We could use design as a strategic advantage. But right now, we don't.

The way we are using design, in many cases, is actually fragmenting our brand image, diluting our differentiation, creating inertia in our system and confusion in the marketplace. We don't use design as a strategic advantage. But we could if we gave it more focus.

We need to design on purpose.

Designing on purpose refers to design that is *strategic*, with a clear connection to strategy; *scalable*, flexible across markets and media; and *inspiring*, using design to build relevance and lead culture.

McDonald's uses design to visualize its business strategy.

McDonald's uses the very clear and consistent "I'm lovin' it" visual identity system (look and feel) to help visualize an integrated business strategy. In its advertising, in-store activations, promotions, and global sponsorships, McDonald's uses design to visually integrate its organization, differentiate competitively and build new love for the brand.

IBM uses design to focus its business strategy.

"When Lou Gerstner arrived at IBM we presented a visual audit to him that demonstrated how IBM was being 'collectively' viewed by our customers. This audit included a representation of how we were presenting IBM in the marketplace, via our logos, advertising, naming, product design, exhibits, publications, etc., the key here being the collective, aggregate-level view. What we found was that because design decisions were being made transactionally, or execution by execution, the result was a fractured presentation of the IBM brand. Customers told us that this fractured visual presentation also sent the signal that IBM was not operating cohesively. That one IBM group did not work with the other IBM group.

"Mr. Gerstner recognized this immediately, and recognized that the same operational problems existed across IBM. As a result, there was a strategic shift in philosophy that emphasized the importance of rebuilding a strong, integrated, single IBM brand and leveraging IBM's collective strengths. Design has played a significant role in that revitalization effort, with a focus on all of IBM's visual expressions."

Lee Green, Director of Identity and Design,

IBM

Apple uses design as *the* competitive differentiator.

Apple is a design icon. Apple sets the standard in using design as a competitive advantage. Every detail matters. Apple creates products that people *have to have* by systematically linking everything back to their growth strategy.

Nike uses design to build reputation.

Nike doesn't make footwear. It creates sculpture that people choose to wear. It doesn't create retail spaces, it creates experiences. From Web-based infotainment to the Niketown door handles, Nike is very serious about using every opportunity to design on purpose. Nike's reputation for design excellence is known worldwide, creating massive brand loyalty and a Goliath-like brand image.

Volkswagen uses design to build culture.

Volkswagen uses design to build a world-class culture (#13 in Forbes' 100 Best Companies to Work For, 2003). Volkswagen uses design to streamline processes making decision-making clearer. It also uses design to create an employee-centered work environment, creating greater employee satisfaction and love for the brand. And that's just the employees. From vw.com, to showrooms to signage to uniform design, Volkswagen consistently uses design to build a cult-like customer culture as well.

Five things we can do to design on purpose:

1. Connect everything we design to our brands.

One way that Apple maintains consistency and leadership is to have a clear idea that is supported by everything it designs—Apple=think different; Nike=personal empowerment; BMW=the ultimate driving machine. We need to clarify the brand idea/proposition for each brand, in plain speak, and use it to drive our design process (in our briefs, concepts and executions).

2. Clearly define visual identity systems for our brands and use them to connect all of our communication tools.

Everything communicates. All too commonly we move from a product or promotion concept very quickly into fine-tuning a prototype design for testing. Once the concept/prototype is tested, we then quickly activate the prototype design elements across point-of-sale, etc. The opportunity to use design to differentiate and build meaning into our brands is much greater than that. To get the most impact and scale, we should clearly define the visual identity system (brand or promotion look and feel) at the strategy stage and then use it to connect all of our communication tools together to create a total brand experience.

3. Create design management tools and guiding principles to ensure a high level of quality across our system.

We need to create clarity for our system by creating tools that make good design decisions easy and bad decisions difficult. We should have standards that take the guesswork (and inconsistency) out of usage of our icons, agency management, and design process flow.

4. Use design to build more consistency between activation programs, licensing, and promotions (both locally and globally).

We can get much more efficiency and create more impact by thinking more holistically about design. The good news is that sometimes we are very strategic with our design. The bad news is that often it is almost by chance and almost never connected to anything else. We could empower a single design steward per brand (global and division-level) to connect brand activation, licensing, properties, promotions, equipment management, etc. to insure that we're leveraging our design opportunities strategically.

5. Link our existing, regional design teams with corporate to achieve better follow-through.

If we linked our design teams together to create a design network, we could leverage our agencies, assets and knowledge much more efficiently and consistently.

The opportunity is huge. The opportunity is now.

Is using design as a strategic advantage an opportunity or our responsibility? We could and should be *the* company that other companies use as *their* standard for great design. We need to design on purpose.

This paper wasn't perfect. In retrospect, it was actually pretty naïve. I have learned so much more about our business since writing it. I now have a much better understanding of just how hard it is to do what I was pushing for. Also, I wish I could say that this is all it takes—a three-page story and a catchy title. Instead, to create systemic change, you have to just keep chipping away— you have to keep linking design to what's important to the company. You have to keep motivating the elephant and the rider.

But you also have to start somewhere. We started by focusing on Coke and a fractured brand identity. Looking back, these five "Designing on Purpose" strategies gave us focus, the "why," but we needed an approach, we needed the "how." We needed to make it easier for people to do the right thing and harder to do the wrong thing. A decade later, we've come a long way, but we're still learning.

The world we live in now is infinitely more complex, even than it was ten years ago, and the stakes higher than ever. But if we can keep the principles of this book in mind—that we must design for agility as well as scale, across the organization—we'll have a fighting chance of celebrating our next hundred years as a brand that consumers continue to love and find relevant to their lives. We wish the same success for you.

Acknowledgments

T HIS BOOK has been a journey. Lots of people say that figuratively; we mean it literally. We've written this book in hotel rooms in South Africa, on a beach in Tel Aviv, in a taxi in Sydney, in a coffee shop in Bangalore, and beside the Bosporus in Istanbul. We prototyped; we iterated; we pivoted. We employed every tactic and cliché you might expect from two people with a big idea together in a garage, if that garage came with frequent flier miles.

One of the most rewarding parts of our adventure was to work with an amazing group of people inside Coca-Cola to capture the story behind each of the cases we relate. So many people contributed to the ideas in this book that it is impossible to list them all here. All we can say is thank you to everyone who made this possible. Hopefully you feel this is as much "your" story as it is ours.

Having said that, we must especially thank Ben Deutsch and Campbell Irving for their staunch belief, patience, and support—and for helping us get to the finish line.

We also owe special thanks to Robert Safian, *Fast Company*'s editor in chief, for the good judgment to assign us the initial story on Coca-Cola in 2009, and then the generosity to give us the time and support to turn it into a book-length tale.

We both are grateful for the help of the talented team at Simon & Schuster, all of whom have been consummate and skilled professionals as well as great people to work with. Emily Loose, Michael Szczerban, and Sydney Tanigawa did heroic work taking a manuscript that had more pivots than a social-app-based startup and whipping it into shape.

And we're especially thankful to have James Levine and the hard-working and dedicated team of Levine Greenberg Rostan Literary Agency on our side. They believed in this idea from the start, and stuck with us unfailingly through the rocky patches and good times alike. We couldn't have done it without them.

This book could not have happened without the help of Ross Berkowitz, Suzanne Berlin, and Ann Stewart. To them, we are profoundly grateful.

Finally, we thank our families, who don't really care about scale and agility, but were gracious enough to listen to us prattle on about this topic during the dinner hour, on road trips, on long walks, and in other places when they'd surely have wished for a conversation about a new film, a good book, or even the pending weather forecast. We're sure they're even happier than we are that this book is finally complete, and they needn't fear another long discussion about the wonders of systems theory. We love them for their endurance and understanding.

DB and LT

Notes

Part 1 Designing for Scale

2 *most of them struggle with scale:* "The No. 1 reason startups fail: Premature scaling," http://www.geekwire.com/2011/number-reason-startups-fail-premature-scaling. Accessed September 1, 2011.

5 *"rather than static snapshots":* Peter Senge, *The Fifth Discipline: The Art & Practice of The Learning Organization* (Doubleday Business, 1990), page 68.

7 *sold for just five cents.* "Why Coke Cost a Nickel for 70 Years," http://m.npr.org /news/Business/165143816. Accessed November 15, 2012.

8 valued at over $120 billion in 2001. *Coca-Cola Company Market Capitalization.* http://www.wikinvest.com/stock/Coca-Cola_Company_%28KO%29/Data /Market_Capitalization.

8 *"Has Coke Lost Its Fizz?"* http://content.time.com/time/business/article /0,8599,227472,00.html. Accessed April 6, 2002.

9 *three-page paper called "Building Brands, by Design."* This document, better known as the "Designing on Purpose" manifesto, is reprinted at the end of the book.

1 Design

15 *Canada from 2007 to 2012.* Stephanie Strom, "Coca-Cola Tests Sweeteners in Battle of Lower Calories," *New York Times,* May 14, 2012.

23 *"that is what it lives with."* Paul Rand, *Design, Form and Chaos* (New Haven: Yale University Press, 1993), page 126.

24 *"behavior over time."* Donella Meadows, *Thinking in Systems* (Oxford, UK: Earthscan, Ltd., 2009), page 2.

25 *signature piece of legislation.* "Err Engine Down," http://www.slate.com/articles /business/bitwise/2013/10/what_went_wrong_with_healthcare_gov_the_front _end_and_back_end_never_talked.html. Accessed October 8, 2013.

26 *"vast majority of users."* Administration: Obamacare website working smoothly. http://www.cnn.com/2013/12/01/politics/obamacare-website/. Accessed July 10, 2014.

28 *80 percent of aluminum cans.* "Should recycling be compulsory?" http://www
.zerowastesg.com/2012/06/05/should-recycling-be-compulsory-news/. Accessed
June 5, 2012.

28 *disappointing 31.5% of its waste.* "Countries with the highest recycling rates."
http://www.aneki.com/recycling_countries.html. Accessed March 25, 2014.

29 *world's priciest cities.* "The 10 Most Expensive Cities in the World," http://m.npr
.org/news/Business/165143816marketwatch.org. Accessed June 13, 2012.

29 *750 square feet.* "House Hunting in . . . Tokyo" http://www.nytimes.com/2010
/03/03/greathomesanddestinations/03gh-househunting-1.html?pagewanted=all
&_moc.semityn.www. Accessed March 2, 2010.

29 *or Australia with 206.* "Average Apartment Size Worldwide | Average Home Size,"
http://www.rentenna.com/blog/average-apartment-size-worldwide-average
-home-size/. Accessed June 19, 2012.

34 *McBaguettes in McDonald's in France.* "Why McDonald's in France Doesn't Feel
Like Fast Food," http://www.npr.org/blogs/thesalt/2012/01/24/145698222
/why-mcdonalds-in-france-doesnt-feel-like-fast-food. Accessed January 24, 2012.

34 *McDonald's in India.* "McDonald's in India: Would You Like Paneer on That?"
"http://www.npr.org/2012/09/23/161551336/mcdonalds-in-india-would-you
-like-paneer-on-that. Accessed September 23, 2012.

2 Scale

38 *Coca-Cola for just one dollar.* Coca-Cola 2010. Anne Hoy, *Coca-Cola: The First
Hundred Years.* (Atlanta: Coca-Cola, 1986), page 38.

45 *"the key to quality per se."* http://www.brainyquote.com/quotes/authors/c/charles
_eames.html. Accessed March 27, 2014.

47 *worth of stuff in 2011.* "Wal-Mart remains atop Fortune 500 List" http://usatoday
30.usatoday.com/money/companies/2011-05-05-walmart-fortune-500_n.htm.
Accessed May 5, 2011.

47 *largest economy in the world.* "Walmart's How Big? What the Huge Numbers Really
Mean," http://www.dailyfinance.com/2011/05/28/walmarts-how-big-what-the
-huge-numbers-really-mean/. Accessed June 6, 2011.

49 *"without ever doing it the same way twice."* Christopher Alexander, Sara Ishikawa, Murray
Silverstein, Max Jacobson, Ingrid Fiksdahl-King, Shlomo Angel, *A Pattern Language:
Towns, Buildings, Construction* (Oxford: Oxford University Press, 1977), page 247.

50 *"patterns which are embedded in it."* http://www.brainyquote.com/quotes/quotes
/c/christophe417065.html. Accessed March 31, 2014.

50 *"web of nature, as you make it."* Alexander. *A Pattern Language*, page xiii.

52 *Jacob's Pharmacy in Atlanta.* Max Pendergrast, *For God, Country & Coca-Cola: The
Definitive History of the Great American Soft Drink and the Company that Makes It,*
2nd ed. (New York, NY: Basic Books, 1993), page 31.

54 *"even if broken, a person could tell at a glance what it was."* Pendergrast, *For God*, page 103.

54 *formed the seed of an idea.* "Birth of a Bottle," http://www.thecontourbottle.com/. Accessed April 28, 2014.

54 *"top like a squash."* "'Real Thing'" Design Based on the Wrong Ingredient," *Miami News*, Friday, May 23, 1986, page 2A. http://news.google.com/newspapers ?nid=2206&dat=19860523&id=h8wlAAAAIBAJ&sjid=TPMFAAAAIBAJ&pg =1315,6312956. Accessed April 28, 2014.

57 *consumer-friendly five-cent price.* Anne Hoy, *Coca-Cola: The First Hundred Years.* (Atlanta: Coca-Cola, 1986), page 13.

3 Complexity

74 *distrust traditional hierarchies.* "7 Surprising Ways to Motivate Millennial Workers," http://2020workplace.com/blog/?p=988, Accessed April 20, 2014.

74 *certain bacteria in our digestive systems.* "The Co-Villains Behind Obesity's Rise," http://www.nytimes.com/2013/11/10/business/the-co-villains-behind-obesitys -rise.html?_r=0. Accessed December 12, 2013.

75 *"business, government and civil society."* "Coca-Cola Announces Global Commitments To Help Fight Obesity," http://www.sustainablebrands.com/news_and _views/communications/coca-cola-announces-global-commitments-help-fight -obesity http://www.sustainablebrands.com/news_and_views/communications /coca-cola-announces-global-commitments-help-fight-obesity.

76 *uses in all its beverages and their production by 2020.* "The Water Stewardship and Replenish Report GRI," The Coca-Cola Company, 2014.

81 *dimensions of the potential upheaval.* "Teen Sells App to Yahoo! for Millions," http://abcnews.go.com/blogs/business/2013/03/teen-sells-app-to-yahoo-for -millions/. Accessed March 26, 2013.

82 *learning instead of education.* "Resiliency, Risk, and a Good Compass: Tools for the Coming Chaos," http://www.wired.com/business/2012/06/resiliency-risk-and -a-good-compass-how-to-survive-the-coming-chaos/. Accessed March 12, 2014.

83 *invasions of privacy.* "Future changes to Facebook privacy settings to be opt-in," http://arstechnica.com/tech-policy/2012/08/future-changes-to-facebook-privacy -settings-to-be-opt-in/. Accessed March 20, 2013.

83 *apartments or houses.* "With Its Latest Hire, Airbnb Gives A Clue On How It's Going To Fight Rental Laws," http://www.businessinsider.com/airbnb-hires -yahoo-david-hantman-2012-10. Accessed May 26, 2013.

84 *"challenges of our time."* Remarks by The Coca-Cola Company CEO Muhtar Kent to the Colorado Innovation Network Summit, Denver, CO, August 29, 2012. Transcript available at http://www.coca-colacompany.com/our-company /muhtar-kents-keynote-speech-at-the-colorado-innovation-network.

84 *but at the center.* M. E. Kramer, "Creating Shared Value: How to Reinvent Capitalism—and Unleash a Wave of Innovation and Growth," *Harvard Business Review*,
January/February 2011.

85 *"left behind so much waste."* Cool Products, Hot Topic: Can EKOCYCLE Inspire
a Social Movement Around Recycling? will.i.am Says Yes. http://www.coca-cola
company.com/stories/cool-products-hot-topic-can-ekocycle-inspire-a-social
-movement-around-recycling-william-says-yes. Accessed April 28, 2014.

85 *Bea Perez, the company's vice president and chief sustainability officer.* http://www
.coca-colacompany.com/press-center/press-releases/an-end-is-a-cool-new-start
-william-and-the-coca-cola-company-recharge-recycling-with-launch-of-lifestyle
-brand-ekocycle.

Part 2 Designing for Agility

92 *cultural myth and meaning.* D.B. Holt, *How Brands Become Icons: The Principles of
Cultural Branding* (Cambridge, MA: Harvard Business Press Books, 2004), page
12.

92 *$1.5 billion in global annual revenues.* "Fact Sheet: Oreo 100th Birthday," http://
www.kraftfoodscompany.com/sitecollectiondocuments/pdf/Oreo_Global_Fact
_Sheet_100th_Birthday_as_on_Jan_12_2012_FINAL.pdf . March 12, 2014.

92 *every company's dream.* "What's Easier: To Make a Billion Dollars, Build a Global
Company, or Create a Global Brand?" http://www.forbes.com/sites/forbes
insights/2013/04/09/whats-easier-to-make-a-billion-dollars-build-a-global
-company-or-create-a-global-brand/. Accessed March 12, 2014.

93 *Louis Vuitton, and, of course, Coca-Cola.* "Billion Dollar Brands," http://www.cbc
.ca/undertheinfluence/season-2/2013/03/09/post/. Accessed March 12, 2014.

96 *lived fast and died young.* "The Path to Epiphany," http://www.cs.princeton
.edu/courses/archive/spring13/cos448/web/docs/four_steps_chapter_2.pdf.
Accessed March 12, 2014.

97 *"a repeatable and scalable business model,"* "A Startup Conversation with Steve
Blank," http://www.forbes.com/sites/kevinready/2012/08/28/a-startup-conver
sation-with-steve-blank/. Accessed April 17, 2014.

98 *in fewer than two years.* "A Year Later, Instagram Hasn't Made a Dime. Was it
Worth $1 Billion?" http://business.time.com/2013/04/09/a-year-later-instagram
-hasnt-made-a-dime-was-it-worth-1-billion/#ixzz2eVAxeFS1. Accessed April 2,
2014.

98 *just couldn't make it work.* "Kodak Buys Ofoto.com," http://www.marketwatch.
com/story/eastman-kodak-buys-ofotocom. Accessed March 12, 2014.

99 *Fourth Era of Innovation.* Scott D. Anthony, "The New Corporate Garage," *Harvard
Business Review*, September 2012.

4 Smarter

102   *even when it wasn't.* "Hmm? Feel that?" http://forums.crackberry.com/general
-blackberry-discussion-f2/hmmm-feel-254716/. Accessed March 13, 2014.

104   *two years too late.* "Once Dominant, BlackBerry Seeks to Avoid Oblivion," http://
dealbook.nytimes.com/2013/08/12/blackberry-to-explore-strategic-alternatives
-including-a-sale-again/. Accessed March 13, 2014.

104   *"the wrong choice and decision paralysis."* "Sustainable Competitiveness," http://
www.weforum.org/content/pages/sustainable-competitiveness. Accessed March
13, 2014.

105   *there are over 700 million.* "Internet 2012 in Numbers," http://royal.pingdom
.com/2013/01/16/internet-2012-in-numbers/. Accessed April 7, 2014.

107   *"Jobs didn't say much, but he agreed."* Walter Isaacson, *Steve Jobs* (New York: Simon
& Schuster, 2011), page 320.

108   *corrosion in nuclear missiles.* "Uses for WD-40," http://www.snopes.com/inboxer
/household/wd-40.asp. Accessed March 13, 2014.

114   *"file in our brain."* "XCD interviews Michael Wolff," http://www.youtube.com
/watch?v=tAeBXIvusVA. Accessed March 13, 2014.

115   *"'company for a while.'"* "The Making of 'I'd Like to Buy the World a Coke,'" http://
www.coca-colacompany.com/stories/coke-lore-hilltop-storyCoca-Cola, Accessed
April 28, 2014.

115   *designed any better.* "Best-ever Advertising Jingles," http://www.forbes.com
/2010/06/30/advertising-jingles-coca-cola-cmo-network-jingles.html. Accessed
March 13, 2014.

115   *"after the campaign stopped."* Jonathan Mildenhall, interview by author, July 9,
2012.

117   *"can hum at work."* Rick Tetzeli, "Portrait of the Rapper as a Young Marketer:
How K'naan Delivered on Coca-Cola's $300 Million Bet," *Fast Company*, October
2010.

117   *"different places," he told* Billboard. "How K'Naan's Song Became Coca-Cola's
World Cup Soundtrack," http://www.billboard.com/features/how-k-naan-s-song
-became-coca-cola-s-world-1004096346.story#plgScxlZJTGTtjy1.99. Accessed
March 13, 2014.

117   *including MoMA in New York.* "Dieter Rams: ten principles for good design,"
https://www.vitsoe.com/rw/about/good-design. Accessed March 13, 2014.

119   *era frozen in time.* Coca-Cola "Glascock Portable Coca-Cola Cooler," http://www
.vintagevending.com/glascock-portable-coca-cola-cooler. Accessed August 22,
2014.

121   *kiosks in their neighborhood.* "Developing Inclusive Business Models: A Review
of Coca-Cola's Manual Distribution Centers in Ethiopia and Tanzania," http://
www.hks.harvard.edu/m-rcbg/CSRI/publications/other_10_MDC_report.pdf.
Accessed March 13, 2014.

121   *definitely did not fit all.* "Slides—Coca-Cola Micro Distribution," http://www
      .thesupplychainlab.com/blog/photo-library/coca-cola-micro-distribution/.
      Accessed March 13, 2014.

122   *finance their new business.* "Coca-Cola Sabco's Inclusive Business Model," http://
      www.ifc.org/wps/wcm/connect/fb3725004d332e078958cdf81ee631cc/
      Coca+Cola.2010.pdf?MOD=AJPERES. Accessed March 13, 2014.

122   *countries change rapidly.* "Slides—Coca-Cola Micro Distribution," http://www
      .thesupplychainlab.com/blog/photo-library/coca-cola-micro-distribution/.
      Accessed March 13, 2014.

122   *90 and 99 percent respectively.* "Coca-Cola Sabco's Inclusive Business Model,"
      http://www.ifc.org/wps/wcm/connect/fb3725004d332e078958cdf81ee631cc
      /Coca+Cola.2010.pdf?MOD=AJPERES. Accessed March 13, 2014.

124   *"justify all that money spent."* "What's Lean about Lean Startup?" http://www
      .agilemarketing.net/lean-lean-startup/. Accessed March 13, 2014.

125   *the bigger the gain.* Nathan Furr and Paul Ahlstrom, *Nail It then Scale It: The En-
      trepreneur's Guide to Creating and Managing Breakthrough Innovation* (Canberra,
      Australia: NISI Institute, 2011), page 68.

126   *"generate more than half of our sales," says Rudolfo E. Salas.* Rudolfo E. Salas, inter-
      view by author, February 13, 2012.

126   *"approaches fourteen times," says Alba Adamo.* Alba Adamo, interview by author,
      February 13, 2012.

5 Faster

136   *"repeatable and scalable business model."* "The Path to Epiphany," http://www.cs
      .princeton.edu/courses/archive/spring13/cos448/web/docs/four_steps_chapter
      _2.pdf. Accessed March 20, 2014.

137   *organizing political protests.* "How Eric Reis Coined 'The Pivot' And What Your Busi-
      ness Can Learn from It," http://www.fastcompany.com/1836238/how-eric-ries
      -coined-pivot-and-what-your-business-can-learn-it. Accessed March 20, 2014.

137   *adapt on the fly.* "The Aha! Moments that Made Paul Graham's Y Combinator Possi-
      ble," http://www.fastcompany.com/3002810/aha-moments-made-paul-grahams
      -y-combinator-possible. Accessed March 20, 2014.

139   *says Coca-Cola design director Tom Farrell.* Tom Farrell, interview by author, De-
      cember 14, 2011.

143   *on the back of a napkin.* "D.Manifesto," http://dschool.stanford.edu/. Accessed
      March 20, 2014.

146   *55 percent of the globe's crops.* "Coca-Cola, Jain Irrigation to showcase modern
      mango farming in Andhra," http://india.nydailynews.com/business/94eee6abc5a
      88d9e8f8d9e47d68be31c/coca-cola-jain-irrigation-to-showcase-modern-mango
      -farming-in-andhra#ixzz2C75FtheZ. NY Daily News. (2012, July 24)

147   *only three to four years.* "Coca-Cola, Jain Irrigation to showcase modern mango farming in Andhra," http://india.nydailynews.com/business/94eee6abc5a88d 9e8f8d9e47d68be31c/coca-cola-jain-irrigation-to-showcase-modern-mango -farming-in-andhra#ixzz2C75FtheZ. NY Daily News. (2012, July 24)

148   *participating farmers double their income.* "2011/2012 Sustainability Report," http://www.coca-colacompany.com/sustainabilityreport/world/sustainable -agriculture.html#section-piloting-sustainable-farming-projects-worldwide. Accessed March 20, 2014.

151   *cases of soda sold in the United States.* "Pepsico Sues Coca-Cola on Distribution," http://www.nytimes.com/1998/05/08/business/pepsico-sues-coca-cola-on -distribution.html. Accessed March 21, 2014.

153   *"The machines call home every night."* Jennifer Mann, interview by author, August 28, 2013.

6 Leaner

163   *he or she owns the system.* "Modular Open Systems Architecture," http://pmh -systems.co.uk/Papers/MOSAoverview/. Accessed April 3, 2014.

164   *potential for things to go wrong.* "Modular Open Systems Architecture," http:// pmh-systems.co.uk/Papers/MOSAoverview/. Accessed April 3, 2014.

164   *sixth-largest economy by 2030.* "Indonesia's foreign economic policy strategy," http://www.eastasiaforum.org/2012/05/14/indonesias-foreign-economic-policy -strategy/. Accessed March 21, 2014.

164   *largest Twitter city in the world.* "Indonesia falls for social media: Is Jakarta the world's number one Twitter city?" http://www.ipra.org/itl/02/2013/indonesia -falls-for-social-media-is-jakarta-the-world-s-number-one-twitter-city. Accessed August 22, 2014.

167   *"we weren't doing today."* "Pop Artist: David Butler," http://www.fastcompany.com /design/2009/featured-story-david-butler. Accessed March 21, 2014.

170   *"move wisdom, learning, and knowledge,"* Joe Tripodi, interview by author, May 7, 2009.

170   *"leadership is doing the right things."* "Do the Right Thing Quotes," http://www .doonething.org/quotes/dotherightthing-quotes.htm. Accessed March 21, 2014.

173   *54 million copies across all platforms.* Minecraft, http://en.wikipedia.org/wiki /Minecraft. Accessed August 22, 2014.

173   *endless variety of gameplay changes.* "How Emergence Changes the Business Model, http://www.gamasutra.com/blogs/KevinGliner/20140214/210808 /How_Emergence_Changes_The_Business_Model.php. Accessed July 14, 2014.

173   *enabled Wilson's project to emerge.* "The United States of Design," http://www.fast company.com/1777599/united-states-design. Accessed March 21, 2014.

175   *answers from actual Zappos employees.* "Zappos Launches Insights Service," http://www.adweek.com/news/technology/zappos-launches-insights-service-97777. Accessed March 21, 2014.

176   *30 to 40 percent that men invest.* "Coke: Advancing Women Will Boost the Bottom Line," http://management.fortune.cnn.com/2012/10/15/coke-advancing-women-will-boost-the-bottom-line/. Accessed March 21, 2014.

176   *women's economic empowerment.* "Coke: Advancing Women will Boost the Bottom Line," http://management.fortune.cnn.com/2012/10/15/coke-advancing-women-will-boost-the-bottom-line/.

177   *shop became a community magnet.* The Coca-Cola Company 2012.

180   *PET packaging by 2020.* "2012/2013 Sustainability Report—"2012/2013 GRI Report," http://www.coca-colacompany.com/sustainability/http://www.coca-colacompany.com/sustainability/. Accessed August 22, 2014.

180   *the world's largest crop.* "Food and Agriculture Organization of the United States, 2009," http://faostat.fao.org http://faostat.fao.org. Accessed August 22, 2014.

180   *gasoline used in the country be composed of bioethanol.* "Cetrel and Novozymes to Make Biogas and Electricity from Bagasse," http://www.novozymes.com/en/news/news-archive/Pages/45620.aspx. Accessed April 18, 2014.

181   *Maine and in Northern Europe.* "Powering Airplanes with Leftover Tree Bark," http://tenthmil.com/campaigns/energy/powering_airplanes_with_leftover_tree_bark.

181   *use algae to produce the materials we need.* Scott Vitters. Interview with the author, December 13, 2011.

182   *grown and harvested sustainably.* "Leading global brand companies join with WWF to encourage responsible development of plant-based plastics," http://www.bioplasticfeedstockalliance.org/news-title-6/. Accessed April 29, 2014.

182   *"products are produced locally," says Scott Vitters.* Interview with the author, December 13, 2011.

182   *20 billion PlantBottle packages in thirty-one countries.* "2012/2013 Sustainability Report—2012/2013 GRI Report," http://www.coca-colacompany.com/sustainability/.

184   *created a Plant-PET technology collaborative,* "Coca-Cola GM of PlantBottle packaging talks new partnerships, future growth," http://www.plasticstoday.com/articles/Coca-Cola-GM-of-PlantBottle-packaging-talks-new-partnerships-future-growth-102420122, Accessed April 20, 2014

184   *the Ford Fusion Energi.* "Driving Innovation: Coca-Cola and Ford Take Plant-Bottle Technology Beyond Packaging," http://www.coca-colacompany.com/plantbottle-technology/driving-innovation-coca-cola-and-ford-take-plantbottle-technology-beyond-packaging. Accessed April 29, 2014.

185   *one created by lean startup guru . . . Ash Maurya.* "Lean Canvas: How I Document My Business Model," http://practicetrumpstheory.com/2010/08/businessmodel canvas/. Accessed April 7, 2014.

Epilogue

189   *how most entrepreneurs build startups.* "The Path to Epiphany," http://www.cs
      .princeton.edu/courses/archive/spring13/cos448/web/docs/four_steps_chapter
      _2.pdf. Accessed April 7, 2014.

191   *that's over 11 million people.* "Who's Starting America's New Businesses—and
      Why?" http://www.forbes.com/sites/cherylsnappconner/2012/07/22/whos
      -starting-americas-new-businesses-and-why/. Accessed April 8, 2014.

191   *startup launches every seventy-two hours.* "Colorado Launches a New Startup Every
      72 Hours," http://www.forbes.com/sites/karstenstrauss/2013/06/10/colorado
      -launches-a-new-startup-every-72-hours/. Accessed April 8, 2014.

191   *startups still fail.* "Reminder: 95 Percent of New Businesses Fail," http://startup
      dispatch.com/startups/reminder-95-percent-of-new-businesses-fail/ Accessed
      April 8, 2014.

193   *"search of its maximum scalability."* "Starting Up versus Scaling Up," http://www
      .forbes.com/sites/groupthink/2013/06/30/starting-up-versus-scaling-up/. Ac-
      cessed April 8, 2014.

The Designing on Purpose Manifesto

207   "When Lou Gerstner arrived at IBM," Brigitte Borja De Mozota, *Design Manage-
      ment: Using Design to Build Brand Value and Corporate Innovation* (Allworth Press;
      New York: 2003) page 136.

Authors' Note

The following are all protected trademarks of The Coca-Cola Company or Coca-Cola subsidiaries within and outside of the United States: ANDINA®, BARQ'S®, BONAQUA®, CAPPY®, CHERRY COKE®, CIEL®, COCA-COLA®, COKE®, COKE ZERO®, CONTOUR BOTTLE™, DASANI®, DEL VALLE®, DIET COKE®, FANTA®, FREESTYLE®, GEORGIA COFFEE®, GLACEAU VITAMINWATER®, HONEST TEA®, ILOHAS®, KROPLA BESKIDO®, LOVE BODY®, MAAZA®, MINAQUA®, MINUTE MAID®, MINUTE MAID MANGO NECTAR®, PLANTBOTTLE™, POWERADE®, PULPY®, QOO®, SPRITE®, CORE POWER®, XMOD®, 5BY20™, DRINK COCA-COLA DELICIOUS AND REFRESHING™, LET'S HAVE A COKE™, OPEN HAPPINESS™, THE COKE SIDE OF LIFE™, and WITHIN AN ARM'S REACH OF DESIRE™.

The following are all protected trademarks of third parties: AERON, AMAZON, AMAZON PRIME, APPLE, BEATS, BLACKBERRY, BOUNTY, BRAUN, CASE-MATE, DISNEY, DURACELL, EKOCYCLE, ENERGIZER, GILLETTE, GOOGLE, JIMMY CHOO, KLEENEX, KODAK, KODAK FILM, LAMBORGHINI, LEGO, LEVI'S, L'OREAL, LOUIS VUITTON, MCALOO, MCBAGUETTE, MCM, MOTOROLA, MUSCLE MILK, NEW ERA, NINTENDO, PAMPERS, PORSCHE, RVCA, SUPER BOWL, TWITTER, UGG, and VISA.

This book is an individual endeavor by its authors David Butler and Linda Tischler. The Coca-Cola Company does not endorse this book nor are its contents a reflection of the overall opinion of The Coca-Cola Company, its shareholders, employees, or executives.

Index

Pages numbers in *italics* refer to illustrations.

About the Authors

David Butler is a discontented designer, relentless learner, and thankful husband and father. He is Coca-Cola's Vice President of Innovation and Entrepreneurship. He's on a mission to make it easier for starters to be scalers and scalers to be starters.

Linda Tischler is an award-winning editor at *Fast Company* magazine, where she writes about the intersection of design and business. In 2009, she originated *Fast Company*'s design website by convincing a team of professional designers to try blogging. CoDesign.com is now one of the web's largest design sites. Her restless curiosity has taken her around the world in pursuit of the most interesting stories and people who are pushing the boundaries in design.

Get email updates on

DAVID BUTLER,

exclusive offers and other great book recommendations
from Simon & Schuster.

Visit **newsletters.simonandschuster.com**
Or scan below to sign up:

Get email updates on

LINDA TISCHLER,

exclusive offers and other great book recommendations
from Simon & Schuster.

Visit **newsletters.simonandschuster.com**
Or scan below to sign up: